ISBN: 978-1-7646514-1-7 (Paperback)
ISBN: 978-1-7646514-2-4 (Hardcover)
ISBN: 978-1-7646514-0-0 (eBook)

Published by Strong Women Publishing

Editing by Edwina Shaw (www.edwinashaw.com)
Cover illustration by Liv Lorkin (www.livlorkin.com)
Cover design by Deanna'sWorld Author Services
Typeset in Merriweather 10pt and Chin Up Buttercup 10pt by Essential Self-Publishing (www.essentialselfpub.com.au)

MY EYEBROWS JUMPED SHIP

by

PATRIZIA SMREKAR

DEDICATION

To my dear Mum
Thank-you for your eternal love and support and for the quotes I will always remember,

'I don't want to have Chinese food anymore. They put too much MCG in it.'*
'I'd like to see if I can buy that book by Bruce Chutney.'
'Don't worry, there's always divorce.'

To my daughter
I know you had no say in it, but I'm forever thankful you chose me to be your Mum. You are the gift that keeps on giving. I love you.

To my best friend, Geraldine
The blessing to have your friendship rain, hail or shine is immeasurable.

To Glyn Howitt and Kylie Clarke
Thanks for your help!

**Melbourne Cricket Ground*

CONTENTS

I couldn't believe what I was seeing. The magnifier was not helping. It seemed as if overnight, the right side of my eyebrows had disappeared. Gone. Missing.

'We'd like to thank our fellow follicles for their support over the years. For enduring wax being poured on them and consequently ripped out. You were all so brutally yanked, pulled, threaded and plucked yet you always came back, stronger than ever. We applaud your dedication, but for now, we're out. Who's joining us?' I hear the hairs say. It must have been a resounding follicular, 'Yes!'

Now I'm left with a look of astonishment, as the left eyebrow holds onto a few hairs, including one rebel that needs to be tamed every day. If the circumstances were different, it would have been removed for insubordination, but given the scarcity of the present resources, I'm loath to eradicate it.

INTRODUCTION

THIS IS ME

This book offers my personal perspectives. The experiences that have shaped my opinions are entirely my own. They don't reflect anyone else's life choices, no matter what form they take.

My narrative is uncomplicated. I come from a conservative, middle-class Italian family in Melbourne. My parents emigrated to Australia from Trieste, a city close to Venice, during the 1950s. We've always been, and continue to be, a loving family. I have a sister nine years younger and I found my all-girls Catholic school experience interesting, most notably during the senior years under the tutelage of nuns. Ethnic finger-pointing was clear. Even with the nicknames "European" or "wog", my physical appearance—tall frame, light brown hair, and brown eyes—helped me fit in.

In the introductory interview for the school, my parents and I were told by the principal to steer clear of a certain group of girls who often got into trouble. Can you guess who became my best friends?

Those girls. In retrospect, our rebellious deeds were tame. We threw eggs on muck up day during the last week of senior school, then known as HSC, and a couple of girls in our group painted, *Be a nun and get none* in bold black letters on the outside of the school building. Undoubtedly this action caused offence to the sisters of the teaching staff. My parents weren't impressed either as all the parents of our class were contacted and asked to financially contribute to the repainting of the wall.

Although Italian, my family didn't conform to the stereotype of making pasta, sauce, sausages or wine at home. We bought it. I grew up seeing wine on the table at lunch and dinner. Before dinner, was *aperitivo time*, and as Mum cooked, Dad and I would share a vermouth on the rocks, a glass of bubbles, or a Campari on ice. I kept this custom alive during my short-lived marriage, as it allowed time to talk about the day, or as in my case, being talked at, by the ex.

Now, at sixty-six, I'm excited about what lies ahead. I value every moment. Focusing on the positives has been beneficial to me. I appreciate the funny side of life. Recent years have brought incredible changes, for which I'm thankful, and I want to share them with you.

I've often expressed to my friends that I don't like people. It's not that I dislike people completely, I find them challenging, and often disappointing. My preferred state is being by myself; I'm a natural introvert.

Sitting at my writing desk overlooking the street below, I watch people go about their daily routines as I take in the smell of brewed coffee from the cafe below my open window. A young mother strolls by with a pram and toddler, an elderly woman walks with a younger companion, an athletic woman jogs, and three schoolgirls lug heavy bags. I see the different stages of womanhood.

Let's chat (mind you, I'll be doing all the chatting), about the trials and joys of womanhood and embrace the journey with the bumps, the lumps, the impatience, the tiredness and everything in between. May my observations about aging bring you a giggle. (No fadoobadahs were harmed in the writing of this book. Ta Kath.)

Will there be judgemental commentary? Most probably. Will there be ridiculous observations? Most certainly. Will there be pontificating? I'd say so. However, consider these comments and observations on life with a degree of skepticism. My goal isn't self-reproach or admitting fault. If I offend anyone accidentally, please forgive me in the spirit of humour!

Let's take the scenic route to sagging gracefully.

XOXO

I'M NOT AN AGEIST, I'VE JUST AGED

These are the observations of the female aging process from an aging female, incorporating the good, the bad, and the not so attractive!

I've penned my observations so that in years to come, I can look back with gratitude for what I had left going for me in my sixth decade. And there's much to be grateful for. I enjoy taking a jab at myself; however, the truth remains that without all the changes, I couldn't have housed a human being within me, nurtured her growth and survived the long hours of motherhood. Womanhood is a challenge, but one I wouldn't change for all the hormones in the world.

Transitioning from a young woman to an older woman is a journey. Each decade holds both fascination and richness, heartache and celebration, however, I've found physical aging the hardest to accept. You could divide these stages into; young woman, woman, mature woman, older woman, old woman and elderly woman. At sixty-six I see myself in the older woman stage. Mine is a visible transition from skinny jeans, tight dresses, shorts and bikinis to wide leg pants, loose dresses, three-quarter length anything and one-piece bathers. It took me the last couple of years to feel relaxed and at ease with the changes in my body. I'm not saying I'm completely happy, but I'm thankful that I've made it to this stage of womanhood.

I try to remain youthful, sans surgery, as I'm too nervous to go down that path. Kudos to those who do. When I sit down and think about this stage of my life, it makes me laugh. What better way to live than laughing through it all?

To Tattoo or Not to Tattoo?

As a child, a woman used to visit our house from time to time. I have no recollection of her name, connection to our family, hair colour, height, family members, or where she lived. My only memory is her eyebrows. A single curved pencil line in an orange brown tone. When she bent down to kiss me, my eyes would dart to her caricatured semblance of eyebrows. I was fascinated with the concept of being allowed to draw on your face.

Only now I can understand the challenges that woman faced in her daily drawing sessions. Over the last year, I've developed an expression that looks perpetually suspicious or disapproving. The once luscious eyebrow hairs on the right side have jumped ship. There are a few hanging on for dear life while those on the left have claimed victory, with a larger number remaining. Now my dilemma is either drawing a reasonable arch every single day or having them tattooed. I'm not great with needles and equally not great with pain, so drawing it is.

In cahoots with the eyebrows, many of my scalp hairs have also gone out in sympathy wanting to try their luck on the bathroom floor, vanity or any other corner of the house. This has caused the occasional, 'Yuck Mum,' as a hair is raised high above a plate of pasta like Simba being presented on Pride Rock. The joys of thyroid, oestrogen and hormonal changes. What treasures are yet to reveal themselves? Only time will tell.

I have discovered that solid framed glasses are the answer to my brow concerns. Migrating from a slim frame to a thicker frame hides the eyebrows. I hope the small rectangular 'granny glasses' don't come back into fashion soon. Glasses are a wonderful accessory and with so many options, it's a great way to add colour and interest to your appearance. Consider buying clear lens options if you don't require them for basic seeing as I do. I also convert sunglasses into prescription reading glasses by switching out the lenses. Now I have a passion for bags, shoes AND glasses. What next?

FOREARMED IS FOREWARNED

Being mid sixty isn't so bad. "It's the new fifties," is a phrase I hear repeatedly. Does subscribing to this theory mean I've gained a decade? I doubt it. This decade's advancement is subtle, almost like a cat stalking its prey. Slowly, stealthily, it gains proximity until the almighty pounce when you glance at your reflection as you're waving goodbye to a friend. Where did that extra arm pendulum come from? Swaying side to side as you try desperately to clench it into position. No matter how hard you try, your upper arm flesh now has the freedom to move about as it pleases.

All those hours of weight training gone! I knew I should have made a more concerted effort with my triceps extensions, bicep curls, triceps kickbacks, dumbbell hammer curls, and the overhead presses. I felt like I was the dumbbell, only managing a couple of these exercises before I couldn't take it anymore. I figured my legs needed the exercise, and my upper arms would be fine the way they were. At one stage during my gym obsession phase, my upper arms were reasonably toned. Now that upper muscle I was so proud of, has slipped under my humerus like a dob of butter oozing down the side of a pancake. Will I need to look at bell sleeves moving forward? Three-quarter sleeves? Are the days of shoe string straps gone? It is certainly looking that way. I pray that someday my upper arms won't stretch so much they look like pieces of dough being held only by fingertips.

PEEK-A-BOO BUM

Today was a crisp, sunny winter afternoon; I thought I'd do some window shopping. I walked past a Seafolly store and admired the gorgeous bikini they had in the window. Stunning autumn tones blending into a deep green background, with some touches of gold. Just my colours. I could see it complementing a tanned, glistening body. I thought for a laugh, I'd try it on. For the colour only.

First, I had to assess if they had the right shape for me. Anything which had maximum cover, please. I needed support in the top and support in the bottom. The top had to have wiring, with not much cleavage showing, otherwise I'm sure I would have a few *udder* looks of disgust! The straps would need the width to cater to the weight. I could see the salesgirl becoming exasperated as she tried to meet my needs, while probably thinking, why did I say yes to today's shift?

I had to accept that the limited options were only going to be even more limited if I mentally blocked out giving them a go. So I went in with great enthusiasm and expectation. I'd make something work. Surely there would be a mix of pieces for me. I suppose the first tragedy was that I had given away the depilatory for the last number of months and I'd forgotten how my pasty white pallor offered zero complement to any colours. The lack of a pedicure certainly didn't help matters. When the girl came to ask if I needed help, I felt like saying yes, but nothing you can help with. Trying on the first bikini was like fitting the Michelin woman for a G-string.

Seriously, when did trying on bathers mean having to find a pair that lifts, supports and clutches everything in? There would be no G-string bottoms, let alone Brazilian cut. My bottom reflects a definite capital W in appearance. Taking into consideration the regular puffy stomach which I've grown accustomed to, a ruche waistline across the body of the bathers would help. I stepped in, yanked up and poured into the second pair. Not too bad. It wasn't until I turned around that I caught a glimpse of the under-hang.

There is a resounding gap in the market for a bather style with super gripping power to hold the lower peek-a-boo bottom. My once younger, well rounded, European derriere now needs serious strapping by a professional. The frequently asked question of years gone by, 'Does my bum look big in this?' has now been replaced with, 'Do these Nancy Janz hold everything up?'. Perhaps cup inserts which assist breast elevation would be an enormous asset in bum hoisting. Bring on the bather bum cups, please!

INVOLUNTARILY NOISES

When did I start emanating grunting noises every time I move? It just crept up on me. I never consciously thought *I'd better grunt as I get up from the chair.* The simplest movements, like standing, bending, or heaven forbid, kneeling, make my joints scream in protest. It's like I'm in a horror movie, sounding like the creaky door opening to the unexpected. The symphony of joints. The problem is that it occurs automatically. I stand up, I groan. I bend, I groan. I kneel, I groan. Only a few movements don't extrapolate that unsolicited noise.

After lunching with a dear friend, she rose from the chair, announcing that sitting for too long was now an issue. The sojourn ended with the complaints, "My back is killing me", and "My arthritis is acting up". I want to know if this will get worse. I think I know the answer.

In five years, will lunch with my friends leave us sounding like a bassoon section?

THE GIRTH

This is a term seldom heard in everyday conversation. Girth, when said with determination, even sounds heavy. GIRTH. A woman's girth delightfully expands as she ages thanks to the glory of hormones. I think I've read every article and listened to every podcast to help move mine, but it now has a life of its own. Uninvited to be part of the rest of my body, it states its claim as the stubborn bulge. The only benefit it provides is that when I look at my profile, it reminds me of my pregnancy thirty years ago. And forget breathing in, I'd be passing out every time I attempted to pour it into my jeans.

Now I understand why they invented the elasticised waist. The exact fashion statement I used to balk at has now claimed its rightful space in my wardrobe. Long ago I was told by a gym trainer that pinching the spare skin around your waistline showed your fat levels. One centimetre was quite acceptable, two centimetres began the quest for reduction, and three demanded immediate attention. He stopped there, short of going into no-go zones. If only I could find him I'd shock him by relaying that if you pinch mine now, there's enough to make rolls of sausages to feed a small Italian village.

My need for girth acceptance only comes by changing my mindset. Therefore, I have accepted the good days and the bad days. On the good days, I will seek a *feel good* outfit consisting of a loose fitting top (not too big, as oversized can create a more damaging visual), and an elasticised waisted pant, or a pair of jeans. On the bad days, I have a selection of loose dresses that, when paired with great accessory pieces, glasses, shoes and handbag, takes the focus away from the girth. Problem solved.

I KNEED TO EXPLAIN

Once upon a time, there were two shapely knees. They proudly exposed themselves throughout in the fashion statements of the seventies and eighties. But as the curtain lowers at the end of a performance, so has my hemline. I'm now at the point of safeguarding the public from exposure to my Shar-pei knees. Holding a pencil in the knee folds is a definite bonus if you find yourself with your hands full. The skin laxity of my upper legs is a timely reminder that I still need to master the skill of pizza dough making. If only I could take a rolling pin and iron out my thigh dough. Suddenly lumps and bumps have sprung up without warning.

I will continue to perspire my way through summer, keeping the public safe from unnecessary feelings of nausea, as I cover up in full length walking gear. As a result, the perspiration has no outlet other than my head. I have never quite understood why my head is the main body part to release any built-up perspiration. After an hour of errands in our

Australian summer, I look as if I have a highly infectious disease and am about to pass out from heat exhaustion or I've just eaten a bowl of jalapeños dipped in Tabasco. If you recall the cartoons where steam comes from ears in anger, my head feels that exact way. People look at me and I know they are questioning why I am outdoors at all. I just need to remember not to mop up the perspiration with tissues. Recently I found myself walking around with bits of tissue stuck to my face, a tribute to Norman Gunston.

IT'S A FINE LINE

My eyesight deteriorating over time is actually a blessing. I looked at myself in the mirror today and took pleasure in the blurry outline of my face. It appears the years have been kind. It's such a shame that once I'd stood there for a few minutes, I needed to get back to reality to make out a clear eyebrow or eyelid. On went the glasses.

Trying to negotiate a curved line with an eyebrow pencil or eyeliner is like filling in a colour by number. Keeping within the lines whilst balancing my glasses is a near impossibility. Therefore, in comes the magnifier. Not just any magnifier, but the strongest – ten-times stronger – that makes you double back when you note the crow's feet, cheek droops, fine lines and jowls. Today my face looks like a pebble has dropped into the middle of my cheek pond and the ripple effect has spread. As long as I stay away from resembling a bloodhound, I'll be most grateful. I think I'll not worry about reading the shop signs as I meander through the arcade this morning. Glasses are off, for now.

I'M ABREAST OF THE SITUATION

Big breasts? Why now? This is a question I keep asking myself. I wanted to buy myself a new knit today. While my boobs were a definite bonus in my younger years, they were never the size they are now. Why on earth do they need to increase in size as we age? Shouldn't they shrink? I know you compress in height thanks to gravity, but enlargement in the bosom holds no benefit.

I'm now searching for a minimiser bra to help camouflage the enlarged protrusions. What is flattering is when I look at my profile, my breasts are on par with my stomach. They used to win but have given up on their post as the hourglass's dominant feature. Let's not mention when the hoist is released. I'm waiting for my boobs to disappear under my armpits once I lie down. Once upon a time, standing to attention was their norm. Now, looking depressed is their assignment. That knit I tried on? I looked as if I'd stuffed two huge cantaloupes into my bra.

Conversations over sleep patterns seem to creep into lunch catch-ups with the girls all too often these days. When I see my friends, it becomes a race to the finish about which one of us has slept the least, woken the most times during the night to pee or spent sleepless hours tossing and turning. It often starts this way.

Gentle Anna; "How did you sleep?"

Isa, a highly competitive person, is always at the starting block. "I only had two hours at most last night."

Sensitive Cathy: "Oh you poor thing. Have you tried chamomile tea before bed?"

"If I did that, there'd be a chance that I'd not even get two hours as I'd need to pee every five minutes!" Isa replied.

"I've been waking up often at night, too. AND I make sure I limit my liquids at least two hours before bed. I read that somewhere. I also read you shouldn't drink too much after midday. Or is that just coffee?" pipes in Elsie.

Elsie would sleep on all fours or in a foetal position if she read it somewhere.

Dear Elsie, I can always count on her quoting some random piece of useless information she read in a doctor's waiting room ten-year-old magazine, or from some odd Facebook page.

"I'm normally asleep for two hours, awake for three and asleep for another three to four." I offer my humble contribution to the race to the finish line.

"Well, I can't get to sleep. At least you get some quality hours. I can't get back to sleep after I get up to go to the bathroom. I wake up every couple of hours. Last night I was awake all night." And the winner is Isa, even though she had just previously told us she managed two hours.

I shook my head, letting Isa know that she'd won, and that I empathised with her terrible situation.

When I arrived home from our lunch, I reflected on how our conversations have gone from being about staying up all night dancing and making out, to complaining about staying up all night.

Once upon a time, we would start getting ready to hit the nightclubs around ten, as the crowds accumulated after eleven. You didn't want to arrive any earlier. It wasn't cool. At least four or five times a week we would bop around till two or three in the morning and then head home before the birds rustled. I was in teacher's college and continued this routine during the first years of teaching as well. I cannot believe I could maintain a professional appearance and attendance while trying for the title of "disco dancing queen". My thanks for the fitness level I achieved goes to Inflation, The Underground, The Metro, The Hippodrome, Chasers, Disco Connection, The Lemon Tree, The Grainstore and others. During the late seventies and eighties, the scene was known for its high fashion, sexual freedom, open drug use and irresponsible alcohol service. I coveted three out of four. Drugs were never my scene. Feeling out of control, didn't sit well with my control freak nature.

Flash forward to today, and I'm yawning at eight pm. It's a rare occasion to be out past ten. I find myself out to dinner, and as soon as nine o'clock hits, I'm thinking about bed, yearning for it as I used to for a secret lover. I'm the Cinderella of bedtime. I admire that she danced until midnight. Today I would have already said, "Thanks so much for the fun night but my bed is calling, no offence," and called for the pumpkin at nine.

If all else is lost, my bed will remain my trusted ally. It never questions my motivation, isn't possessive, and is reliable and accessible at any time. What's this change all about? A bed is a bed, correct? I've been relying on one all my life. But never like this. In my youth, bed was the last place I wanted to be, but now if I could take all my meetings and meals in bed, I'd be a happy camper. I now understand the concept of a sit-in. Mine is a lie-in like John and Yoko's, though without the sex and I'm not protesting anything. Only that I can't get to bed early enough.

Perhaps the restlessness in our sleep patterns today results from too many years of fun? Instead of dragging my sore feet home at three am after a night of Donna Summer and Gloria Gaynor, I'm now trying to keep my feet still at three am and return to sleep. It's interesting how human physiology states that we return to infancy. My thinking is that my present sleep patterns reflect those of a toddler. Waking early, going to bed early and napping during the day. I am waiting for the progression to nappy wearing, which is a joy that may be bestowed upon me sooner than later!

CHIPS VERSUS CHOLESTEROL

Chips and red wine have always been my favourite pairing. This combination conjures up a fluffy white rug in front of a crackling open fire on a cold winter's night. I watch a lot of movies. The best I can muster is a short-haired throw in front of the YouTube open fire on my TV screen. It crackles somewhat and when I turn on the heater above the screen; it sort of works. Unfortunately, my cardiologist doesn't see my vision.

My warm, comforting visual blew up into tiny shards of despair. Why did he have to specify two drinks a week? Now that number haunts me every time I think of cocktail hour. It would be easier to sleep through five days a week and have two drink nights. If I abused my privileges in my earlier years, I'd understand, but now I'm being reprimanded for being careful. I think I'll invest in an air fryer but I'm loathe to convert to zero alcohol red wine. Tried it once, and it tasted like diluted vinegar. I can only do so much.

Whatever possessed me to agree to having a cat in the apartment at my age? Please explain! My daughter returned home from living overseas and to help her settle back after a seven-year absence, I redirected her conversations about getting a cat into, "Why don't we foster some kittens instead?" The Lort Smith is a wonderful institution that fosters and adopts out cats and dogs and is also an animal hospital. Perfect, I thought. We had fostered three kittens many years earlier, and we both loved the experience. Back then, my error was taking in those foster kittens while we already had a cat. Their presence annoyed her, escalating over two weeks despite my keeping them separate, culminating in our cat's hunger strike. I understood that depression had set in and therefore returned the fluffy bundles of absolute cuteness. They were then adopted. With every trace of the outsiders gone, our cat's spirit revived, and she returned to her healthy self once more. It's fascinating how sensitive cats can be.

I was overjoyed at the chance to foster again, giving my daughter and me the freedom to cherish our favourite animal without any strings attached. However, unexpectedly, we were given four kittens, including an adorable runt, tiny enough to fit into my palm. When it came time to return them after eight weeks, the runt had developed a raspy cough due to a mishap during his de-sexing. The Lort Smith told us he would need to be euthanised. We could not see that happen.

Now, after seven months, I can carry him around my neck like a fur stole. I've always been a cat lover. My daughter wanted total responsibility, which I welcomed. However, she has taken herself overseas for a month and I'm left babysitting the cat. I've made every effort to ensure his comfort, even to the point of letting him sleep on my bed. Unfortunately, what was a rare decent night's sleep has now become an interrupted interlude.

Between waking to the deep breathing noises, or a paw in my face, he has now decided clawing his way up the fabric bedhead pre-dawn is a fun activity. The finale to this act is to perform a flying kamikaze onto the bedside table. As a result, my bedhead now resembles a laundromat with items of clothing strewn all over it to dissuade his assent to the top. When I note his pupils have dilated to the maximum extent, Boba eyes, I know the assent is imminent. He has also taken to eyeing off the height of my periwinkle velour drapes. I know that can't be good. As he sits on the carpet staring upward, I can hear the calculations going on in his brain. *These things must be at least two to three metres high. If I make a concerted leap, I could claw my way to the top. I guess a back-flip with a half twist onto the bed is the way to land it.*

It's just a matter of time!

From now and until my daughter's return, I'm going to close the bedroom door, leaving him the rest of the apartment as a playground and pray I will find the lounge room in some sort of recognisable shape in the morning. In hindsight, an adult cat of advanced age may have suited me, as we'd be seeing eye-to eye.

DRIVING MISS CRAZY

Today I was conscious of the cars around me as I drove to the Chadstone shopping centre. There's a new section of road where the gigantic, triple-decker, alien-looking road- churning trucks drive so close that if I were in the passenger seat, my fingers would be burrowed deep into the dashboard.

When I was younger, I'd zip around in a little Mitsubishi Dad bought for me at a bargain price. That it only had one airbag didn't seem to deter his purchase. Now I have a sturdy German machine, a Mercedes. It rings, beeps, flashes and has park assist. The more bells and whistles, the better. I've worked out that I used to focus on the road ahead when I was a younger driver. Now I focus on the cars beside me, fearing that at any time one could come hurtling into my lane, or cut in front. It's the fear of something going wrong which plagues me. And night driving? Prefer not to, thanks. My eyes are okay but I concentrate so much it's as if I'm threading a needle each trip.

I accept Uber is now my friend. I'm

guessing these paranoiac thoughts come in multiples as I'm also a nervous flyer, which I wasn't before. Added to the list is the fact that I slipped on a piece of banana and broke my knee a couple of years ago, so now I'm also fearful of falling. I would have been well suited to the ancient Egyptian days, being carried around in a palanquin. Cleopatra, you're my inspiration!

HEEL OR NO HEEL, THAT IS THE QUESTION

I've just come home from a great cocktail function. I wore a lovely bottle-green mid-calf dress, cinched at the waist. The only appropriate shoe for this length is a heel. If you wear a flat shoe, you might as well give up on all attempts to look as if you have legs.

The shoes I chose have a ten-centimetre heel with a pointed toe. I decided I'd brave them after not having worn any high heels for a long time. Gorgeous if I was going out TEN YEARS AGO! However, I felt it was like riding a bike. I'd be fine.

Within the first thirty minutes, I showed a decent smile to the guests I was chatting with. The worst part was I was a special guest and being continually introduced to others. The people must have thought I had a serious UTI as I kept excusing myself to use the bathroom. All I could think of was sitting down for a bit. My feet were throbbing, my bunions screaming to be let out and what's more, the random few seats available were occupied by people in orthotic shoes. I would have given anything to swap with them.

I thought standing still was the best option, so I found a bar table where I could lean and lift one foot at a time to gain some temporary relief. Unfortunately, I gave the impression the table was holding me up and a couple of guests kept asking if they could get me a coffee. Those shoes are now with the Salvos.

I WANT TO SAY IT AS IT IS

I need to make selfishness an asset. I keep hearing that as you get older, you become more self-centred. I'm waiting to throw myself into this project. Will I finally be able to say, "It's been great seeing you, but I think we've exhausted all areas of interest." Wouldn't that bring a smile to my face? At this stage in my life, it's important to nurture being irritable and cranky. All I've done up to date is help, support and nurture others, be they friends or family. That's been fine, no complaints. But now I'd like to express what I'm thinking.

I'd like to jump all queues, ask slower walkers to move aside, return any food orders which are not up to my standard, not hold the lift for anyone and not allow any drivers in when they try to jump the queue. Plus, I'd like to tell elderly citizens they could have thought of opening their wallet ahead of time while the bread was being packaged instead of waiting until it's been placed in front of them to rummage around putting together the

ten and twenty cent pieces to pay for it.
The art of being cranky.

CANCER PROVIDES NO BENEFITS, OR DOES IT?

What if I told you there is a positive spin to everything in life if you look for it? Well, this morning I was reminded of mine. My dearest friend, ten years younger, called me to complain about the horrendous night sweats she's been experiencing. I empathised with her, of course, then after the phone call, I sat down and reminisced about my hot flushes.

I was forty-six at the time of my diagnosis and I was in shock, as all people are at receiving such devastating news. Mine was bowel cancer. *That really sucks,* was my first thought. It hits you in a surreal way. So many questions come to mind and yet my mind went blank. My doctor told me, that because of the radiation therapy, *I'm so sorry, but you will go into immediate menopause.* After digesting that piece of information, I spun it around. Really? And that's a bad thing? No more periods? No more cramps? No more crabby mood swings? No more piles of sanitary equipment clogging up my bathroom cabinets? So my thinking changed to, *I'll eliminate all the monthly inconveniences for the next ten years for a few weeks of radiation therapy*? Yes! Plus, the bonus is it will help cure this bastard of a thing. I see no negatives.

As a huge fan of Bugs Bunny, the following event made me feel like I was living in an episode. One Saturday morning around eleven, I was walking on the ground floor of Doncaster shopping centre towards a café, enthusiastically expecting to join Mum for a coffee. As I approached, I could see her back and I focused on that. Suddenly my right foot took off straight in front of me, allowing no time to regain my balance, but forcing my left knee to bend and hit the marble floor with full impact. The front part of my sneaker had slipped on a piece of banana, which had been camouflaged by the coffee-coloured flooring right in the middle of the busy shopping centre. Only in cartoons do you see a character with their legs flying into the air and landing on their bum. But in my case, on a bent knee. The long and painful healing process involved having to wear a full leg brace and hobble around with crutches. Whereas Bugs always made a miraculous and immediate recovery.

As I lived on my own, it made for

some hilarious visuals. Picture this, as Sophia Petrillo from the Golden Girls would say. At one in the morning on a Sunday, in a deep sleep, I heard a beep, but ignored it, thinking I was dreaming. Beep again. And again. Pillow held tightly around my head was useless. Beep. Beep. Beep. The stupid smoke alarm. I had no choice. Dragging my left fully braced leg into the cold air, I grabbed the crutch beside the bed and started belting the smoke detector. I was going to smack it off the ceiling until I thought of the aftermath that would create. I knew the battery had to come out. So, the circus act began.

The only chair I had to stand on swivelled. Picture me in my leg brace climbing onto this chair, desperately trying to balance as if on a tight-rope, swivelling left and right, as I made attempts at flipping open the smoke alarm. Beep. Beep. Beep. Those earlier years of dance came in handy. Doing the twist on a swivel chair with a broken leg in a full brace would have been one of the most stupid things I've ever done. But sleep deprivation would have been worse.

⁘ THE CLOSETED CLEANSE ⁘

Today I felt empowered to bring some pieces of clothing out of the closet. It's been a long time since I assessed what I had in there. Once I sat on the bed and stared at my open wardrobe, I realised I had to approach the job with determination. I would not allow any piece to re-inhabit the abyss, unless it could prove its worth. The theorists would have you take everything out and lie it on the bed, then put each piece back if it fits well, is in great condition and has been worn in the last year.

The bed is piled high with clothes, some of which haven't seen daylight for several years. They are steadfast and loyal and will not relinquish their place. I begin with the top dress which has been in there since my 27-year-old daughter was in junior school. I test the theory. It fits, still looks in decent condition. Back it goes. I proceed through the next ten pieces and find they all fit into the same category, so back they go as well. By the time I break for coffee, I realised that the only outcast is a tank top with unravelled stitching. Success.

Taking the coffee back with me, I sat on the bed and reassessed. I reframed the question. Which pieces are you sick and tired of dragging out of this sorry closet each year? Out of the 59 items originally housed, 20 now remain, trusted and loyal. Theorists indeed.

MASTERCHEF, NEVER

Once upon a time, I was known as the risotto queen. That was and still is my favourite restaurant dish. Mushroom risotto was my specialty to cook at home. Using a mix of dried porcini mushroom added to button and portobellos, made for a tasty Italian dish. Mix in a generous dob of butter and add a good handful of Reggiano grated parmesan at the end of the cooking process. Let rest for a few minutes and the result is a risotto of creamy consistency. Delicious.

Things have changed and if there's one thing I hate doing now, it's cooking. Many years ago I did my fair share of it, raising my daughter and feeding an ex-husband. I find eating is a need to only. You won't ever find me mulling over a recipe, painstakingly compiling a list of ingredients, contending with the supermarket bustle, the heavy bags I must trudge home and unpack, all before I can even begin. Please! A packet of pre-washed lettuce with a can of tuna sprinkled on top will do the trick. Don't get me wrong, avid cooks and chefs out there, I tip my lack of chef's hat to you. I admire your tenacity and dedication to your art.

The kitchen, for me, is a place to get in and out of quickly. No need to open cupboards, stand contemplating what genius concoction I can extrapolate from the ingredients. Just start with a G and T and Twisties, open the can of soup followed by a ham and cheese toastie, finishing with a scoop of raspberry vanilla ripple. What more can you ask for? I've saved a ton of money on cooking lessons.

MINIMALISM IS NEAR IMPOSSIBLE TO REACH

I think I'm a little obsessive. I've watched these YouTube people talk about how to achieve a minimalist lifestyle. One I would love to harness. I am on the eternal journey of throwing things away. Mind you, I'm very sustainable where possible, so I can justify the throwing. The problem is that even though this happens regularly, the phenomena of both the accumulation and resurgence of stuff continues even with minimal buying.

A few months ago, my "Sex and the City shoe room" (I wish), was converted from a study holding all my shoes, bags and accessories in pristine order, to a sound studio for my daughter. Now my cupboards are crammed. Everything which was out, is now in. I seriously have to reduce the number of shoes I possess. I think I have a sickness. *Shoe obssessia.* Then there is the exhaustion at looking at the utensils drawer and seeing four scrapers, three whisks, six champagne stoppers (these DO come in very handy mind you) and copious numbers of tools

I've rarely used, or need to look up how to use, is frustrating.

It doesn't take a MasterChef kitchen to open a can of tuna and drop it on some lettuce. But the persistent thought that I may need that odd object someday lingers. It drives me crazy. As for the bathroom cupboard, it's jammed with all sorts of lotions and potions. I've pleaded with my family not to give me anymore body lotions for Christmas. I have enough to smear myself and get down a twenty-meter slide ten times over AND with no abrasions.

IS MARRIAGE REALLY NECESSARY?

I find it extraordinary that some people still deem marriage a vital part of a woman's life, at any age. The marriage question still becomes part of discussions with the girls. *Don't you want to marry again? I'm sure you'll get married. Don't give up hope.*

Hope? I hope I don't need to wash any other man's dirty undies or listen to him snore, while I toss and turn, heaven forbid, or see him walk around in his full glory, unless he's worth seeing. The last thing I need is, *What's for dinner? Can you make this?* I have become used to my space, so much so, that even the cat has now been redirected to snoozing in the lounge room as he was cramping my sleep. I guess the difference is that being told by the girlfriends, *You don't want to be alone* is different from telling people *It's okay to WANT to be alone.*

I enjoy good company, great laughs and loud music. That trio can contribute to a great night out. But at this age, I don't want to contend with irate ex-wives and difficult situations. So, woo me all you want, but don't expect a guaranteed house-cleaner, cook and social worker.

I'M FINDING IT HARD TO TOLERATE BEING INTOLERANT

Tonight, we celebrated my friend's birthday. It was a lovely restaurant and given this, the waiter kindly asked if there were any food intolerances. It takes a waiter at least one if not two trips to the kitchen to check with the chef after I tell him I'm lactose, fructose and wheat intolerant. I can sense the *Why did you sit at my table*? Even though they are being very pleasant. It annoys me I need to advise waiters that I can't have this or I can't eat that. I prefer to gauge where the bathroom is situated and just order. I feel all eyes on me as I keep prolonging everyone's ordering.

The elasticity of the fabric worn is another important factor to the success of an evening. My outfit has to allow for maximum expansion or at least be loose-fitting to cover the inevitable swim ring which will appear by the end of the night.

POSITIVE VERSUS NEGATIVE THINKING

I've always seen myself as a positive person, strong and determined to find solutions to problematic situations. I find the philosophy of, *You're as old as you feel*, laughable. Let's be realistic; will saying I feel ten years younger actually help me? My bunions don't allow me to wear high heels, my waistline has expanded to exclude slim fitting dresses, and my reduced enjoyment of night driving, along with a penchant for early nights, prevents me from feeling ten years younger. I think the best solution is to admit that I am sixty-six years old and loving it. This way of thinking has gotten me through till now and apart from regular visits to my cardiologist, endocrinologist, physiotherapist, gynaecologist and oncologist, I can be thankful for the rest. That reminds me, I need to book my colonoscopy.

I NEED TO BE COMMITTED

This morning, I did what many other women this age may have done. I looked in the bathroom mirror and stretched my cheeks back. Mm, yes, that would make a vast improvement. But could I ever face plastic surgery? A television reality star I have followed over the last two years now has a mouth resembling the joker from Batman. Any tighter and she would look like a muppet when she speaks, mouth stretched from ear to ear. The problem is that you can't just try plastic surgery. For once you see yourself looking good, how can you say you'll go back to looking worse? So, it becomes a commitment.

As I cannot even commit to ingesting my regular daily vitamin tablets, I think I would be a miserable failure at committing to surgery. I don't think I could stand the confusion my friends and family would face. *Didn't she look great at Xmas! What's happened to her between then and Easter?* I think I'll stick to the term 'aging naturally', rather than aging gracefully.

THE RIGHT WORDS

Why am I having such difficulty finding profound and lasting lessons to teach my daughter? Moving beyond the philosophical ideals of self-determination and financial freedom; I've never thought of any other magnificent words to impart. *Make sure a man never defines who you are and that you have your own financial independence.* So many movies show beautiful mother-daughter connections, making me wish I could create a similarly life-changing occasion. However, the painstaking effort put into crafting those scenes shows the impossibility of reproducing these moments in real life.

Reflecting on my past relationship with my mother, I recall some wise advice she gave me. Seeing my wedding rehearsal anxiety, she offered this comforting (albeit unconventional) advice: 'Don't worry, there's always divorce.' So reassuring.

THE MAN OF MY DREAMS, MY CAT

I've had a frank and introspective look at my past relationships and now understand why I love my cat so much. At this stage in my life, he embodies all I desire in a man. He is welcoming when I get home, makes me feel loved and adored, is ready to play when I am, will eat when I'm ready and cleans up after himself. Unquestioning and undemanding, he accepts my decisions. No need to explain where I'm going or where I've been. To top things off, he will sleep beside me expecting nothing and if he cramps my style, I can simply nudge him.

My royal cat. He doesn't complain and I don't have to explain. The perfect partner.

DOGGONE IT!

People walking their dogs caught my attention this morning. It's true that some dog owners look like their dogs, or the other way around. I thought about what dog breed I most resembled. I'd need one with long legs, a rounded middle, longish snout, soft to touch and an introverted personality. Perhaps a dachshund and greyhound mix? Might be a tricky breeding situation, however. But if the greyhound can splay his legs, we may have a winner.

SENSE OF HUMOUR

Why do some people have it and others don't? It's an intriguing thread to pull. *She won't get it; she has no sense of humour.* How many times have I heard that? Don't they laugh at silly jokes? Or at least break out into a giggle? How about cats doing funny stuff or *Funniest Home Videos*? Anything? What brings this about?

Much of our sense of humour is shaped in childhood. Does having a lack of humour growing up or being surrounded by non-funny family and friends influence one's sense of humour, or lack thereof?

I was brought up by a father who liked sarcasm and while that can be offensive, it can also be amusing. The comedy shows on television throughout my youth were clever, dry and entertaining, so I will deduce from my personal experience that comedy is a learned skill.

Being funny is a way of thinking that differs in people. I find English, American and Australian humour to be different from each other. All offer a breadth of clever, intelligent and simple forms of making us laugh. During my younger years, inappropriate comedy was acceptable and it's incredible to see how humour has changed and evolved into a far more conservative way of entertaining. While I agree on most nuances and mechanisms to cope with life's absurdities, we need to be careful not to strip all the fun from life's experiences just to benefit a few people. We need to always laugh at ourselves and with others too.

OCTOGENARIAN

I have a hunch that I'm going to be a grumpy octogenarian. The other morning, I found myself at my favourite cafe, my writing haven, in peaceful quietude. An elderly woman waited patiently while her companion chattered away on her phone. Following the call, she remained engrossed in her phone, constantly scrolling, writing, and scrolling again. At some point, the person showed the screen to the elderly lady, who responded with a polite smile. The interaction was short-lived. Her friend returned to the phone, while the elderly lady sat silently, relishing every mouthful of a small pastry.

I'm often impressed by the patience of some of our elderly citizens. They hold back until everyone else has finished their conversations, calls, and coffee. I get it; they have nowhere to rush, but I doubt I'll sit that quietly. I doubt I will remain patient while trying to adjust to everyone's schedules. I struggle with it now; I can't you imagine how I'll be in fifteen years?

I'll reach the point where I'll have to threaten singing loudly to get you to put the phone down. I hope I won't have to bust out the Elaine dance from Seinfeld. (If you're unfamiliar with it, I suggest you google it.)

Any chance of hitting ninety? Do you become fearless when you're in your nineties? From my experience with two family members who lived to ninety and one-hundred and two respectively, I've observed that people become self-absorbed later in life. Ninety is when the requests begin. *Do you mind if? Could you pick up a? If you have a moment, could we? I don't mean to bother you, but...*

I follow a magnificent woman on Instagram. She is eighty-two and very well put together, her make-up is on (I suppose you need to being on camera), the clothes are bright, the nails are done; the sunglasses are big. Nikki Haskell has life lessons to share. There is nothing like passing on wisdom, regardless of whether you agree with her or not.

Another incredible woman, Iris Apfel, quipped, "Get old, but don't get boring." She lived to the amazing age of one hundred and two, passing away in March 2024. I admired her, as a renowned interior designer, entrepreneur, and fashion model in New York who debuted later in life. A strong and talented woman who kept her business acumen and strong fashion sense till the end. She designed and wore fabulous big framed glasses. As my role model, she has given me something to strive for. Grand bi-fo-cals a la Elton John.

BOOBY PRIZE

While lounging on the couch reading today, I discovered I could use my sixty-six-year-old hormone-enlarged breasts as a makeshift shelf for my cup of tea. Handy....

NO POOPING

This morning, on my walk, I noticed that a long strip of green grass running parallel to the footpath had been trimmed and manicured. In the middle of one section was a ten by six centimetre sign with a squatting dog with the words, "Please pick up after your dog."

A lady ahead of me was walking her terrier. The dog was leading the way until they reached the sign. As if on cue, the dog did his circling, then squatted to relieve himself. I laughed. How did he know? The owner might've thought of leaving, but the dog waited, its stance implying, *Well? Clean it up! Can't you read?*

Yesterday, I was in my home clothes when my daughter was unexpectedly called away to work. Her Uber mistakenly took an alternate route, driving past before turning down the road. I'm not sure how they managed that, considering they have road maps and GPS guidance. I was called on to rescue her from the potentially disastrous late arrival and raced to get my car.

"Just need to put other pants and shoes on," I said, my tone alerting her to my stress levels.

"Don't worry, Mum, you're not getting out of the car."

Regardless, I couldn't leave the house in pyjama pants and slippers because, well, you never know. What would happen in an accident or if I got a flat tyre? Was this anxiety? My thoughts wandered to scenarios and "what ifs" that many people don't think about. Part of the reason may be my teaching career, which demanded constant vigilance and responsibility for young children's well-being. There were constant *what ifs*. I hope to become someone who is more relaxed and accepts that not everything can be predicted. I've been working hard to follow this policy. It takes practice to keep telling oneself, *Chill*. Baby steps.

Later that day as I was walking down a quiet street, a car stopped, parked, and an older woman got out wearing only a nightgown, short robe, and slippers. She obviously doesn't believe in the *what ifs* theory.

PALPITATIONS- BE STILL MY BEATING HEART

I've been experiencing elevated heart rate after going through menopause. Have you ever experienced that sensation when your heart feels like it's in your throat and either skipping a beat or racing too quickly? It's terrible because you can't predict if it will stop or result in a complete cardiac arrest. To safeguard my health, I felt it best to see a cardiologist right away to start monitoring my condition. Yes, he discovered two "loose" valves, as I like to refer to them, but there was "nothing to worry about", he said. Despite this, the flushing and palpitations continued.

I regularly start my mornings by going out for coffee, where I read the newspaper and attempt to begin my day serenely. Mind you, half the articles you read would cause massive palpitations if you take in all the car crashes, home invasions, inflationary prices, electricity costs, world unrest, domestic violence, ambulance ramping problems, knife attacks and... I could go on. After consuming three to four cups of coffee throughout the day, partly due to old habits from the school staffroom, I would lie in bed, contemplating the cacophony of thoughts in my restless mind. Interrupted sleep and watching world news in the middle of the night was possibly not the best habit.

One morning about five months ago, I rolled out of bed, puffy eyed from lack of sleep and hair resembling a cross between a faux fur throw and a spiky echidna, and headed to the cafe. I used a bronzer to conceal my pale face to prevent any resemblance to a zombie from *The Walking Dead* and started reading the paper. My eyes went straight to an article about a couple who survived a home invasion carried out by four children aged between eleven and sixteen. I closed the paper, put it back for another patron to peruse and ordered myself a decaffeinated coffee.

As I sat back and relished the coffee, I realised there was a minimal difference in taste or aroma. I was bracing myself for a headache because of caffeine withdrawal, but I was surprised when this didn't happen. Change this scenario, I thought. Reinvigorated, I settled and enjoyed scrolling through entertaining Instagram posts instead, while coming up with random witty remarks to add to my notebook. That day I started forming new habits. It brought to mind George from Seinfeld, who during a scene, ordered the opposite of what he would normally do at Monk's Cafe, as everything in his life had been a series of mistakes until that point.

The waitress approached the booth and confirmed George's habitual order. "Tuna on toast, coleslaw and a cup of coffee?"

George responded, "Nothing has ever worked out for me with tuna on toast. I want the complete opposite of tuna on toast. Chicken salad on rye, untoasted, with a side of potato salad and a cup of tea."

Could the opposite also be a viable option for me? I restricted my paper reading to weekends when there are more captivating and diverse articles, and made a habit of drinking decaffeinated coffee every day, either at home or out.

I seldom experience palpitations anymore. Rare occurrences no longer concern me, allowing for more occasional restful sleep. My mother, who is a devoted reader of the newspaper and watches the news every night, deserves credit for changing my mind-set. When I take her out, the first thing she talks about is everything that is going wrong in the world. It's all right if you prefer to focus on the negatives, but I've decided not to get caught up in that mind-set anymore. In no time, I'll transform into a senior citizen who is old and grumpy. There's plenty of time to wallow in all that is wrong. For now, I'm going to focus on the positives and keep that heart ticking calmly for as long as it can.

HOW DID I BECOME MY DAUGHTER'S PUBLICIST?

My daughter and I were taking a lovely European vacation together a few months ago with so many gorgeous cities, architecture and history to enjoy. There were memories to capture, moments to savour, sights to behold, flavours and tastes to share and experience.

That's fine to take in for a moment and then the question arises, "Can you take a photo of me?"

"Sure," I say and I accommodate.

But you see, it's not just a photo, it's a paparazzi frenzy of snaps that need to be perfectly centred, lighting appropriately visualised, poses flawlessly actioned and after all that, we might have one worthy shot. In the meantime, it's a barrage of criticism of not seeing the balance, too much leg, don't include the legs, not close enough, too far, centre it properly, I look awful and more! The stress and pressure of creating the picture-perfect photo takes away not only my phone storage, but increases the fear of coming across another "perfect" photo op.

I might stay in the hotel room from now on.

To Be or Not to Be, By Myself

I cannot remember the last time I took some days for myself. There is always a reason to not do what I so desperately want to do. But surely in retirement I can choose what I want to do, when I want to do it, and how I want to do it.

I took it upon myself to attend a writers' festival in Tasmania. I booked a four-day getaway, which I thought would be fabulous. I went on a plane by myself, decided what and when to eat by myself. I meandered around the shops by myself and snacked in bed watching re-runs of *I Love Lucy*, all by myself. That was the clincher. They could have been discussing the positive effects of manure on cabbage fields at the festival, as far as I was concerned. The overarching benefit was being by myself.

I love company, don't get me wrong, but at present having an adult daughter at home, an ailing ninety-year-old mother to assist and care for, plus keeping the house in reasonable order, and the cat, that's a pretty full agenda.

I was welcomed home by dishes on

the kitchen bench-top, extras in the sink, empty food boxes on the island bench and both the rubbish and recycling bin so full that had I not transferred it immediately into a bigger bag, it would have exploded all over the floor. So much for leaving the rubbish as it was when I left, because of my rushed morning commute to catch an early flight, thinking that my daughter would surely take care of it. Had I stayed away for several weeks, I'm sure I would have walked in on an episode of *Hoarders*, opening the front door and pushing aside piles of empty receptacles and refuse strewn all over the floor, as I skidded in calling, "Is anyone still alive?"

Over the years, I have become more arachnophobic than ever. As a single mum, I had to put on a brave face whenever there was an intruder of the six or eight-legged type. My daughter became increasingly concerned about the eight-legged ones. She didn't want to talk about them, let alone see them. So, I made sure I treated any incident casually. "I'll just get the spray and handle it. We are bigger than they are, remember," was my mantra. "But they can jump," was hers. Today I freeze when I come across a spider. It makes my skin crawl even writing the word. I've gone so far as to book a pest control company to come and eradicate any semblance of the tiniest of creatures from the apartment. That, I believe, is money well spent.

Last year I was at the kitchen island bench preparing dinner, music blaring as I grooved along to the Smooth Vintage radio station, which plays seventies and eighties hits, my favourite memory jerkers. Patrick Hernandez, "Born to be Alive" came on. As I was swaying side to side, knife in hand, chopping carrots, I glanced up to appreciate the magnificent sunset view through my glass balcony doors. Right at that point, I saw a huntsman the size of a glove race diagonally across the glass and disappear into the right-hand corner. It moved so quickly that if I hadn't looked up at that very moment, I would have missed it. The issue was now, was it on the inside or the outside of the glass? I couldn't make that out from far away. I froze. My brain went into overdrive. *What do I do? What do I need? A shoe? Broom? Someone else?* All came to mind, but I was on my own.

I have been known to empty a whole can of bug spray on one small spider gripping to dear life on the ceiling, with liquid forming a mini waterfall post death, more like a drowning. So, spray in hand, a full can mind you and a shoe in the other, I approached. I feared looking up into the pelmet area as some time ago I had spotted another spider, hunched into a ball, trying to evade my glance. This time, nothing. No sign of it. Then the terror of it being somewhere else along the wall, floor, or rug. *Lord, please help my vision be sharp.* I pushed my glasses up. Nothing.

At that point, I was ready to call off dinner and move to a new apartment. The only thing I could console myself, was that the spider must have been on the outside. It had to be. Sliding the balcony door across slightly to see if I could spot it in the corner. Again, no luck.

The pest control company was going to come the following week. I moved the appointment forward.

I CAN'T REMEMBER

Something I wish I could change? My memory. I have a poor memory. My whole life, I've heard the words—*it's strange you have no memory of it, isn't it?* I attempt to recall whatever it may be, but I can't. I'm envious of people my age, and younger, who can easily remember statistics and facts. They read books, then recall in detail the characters and story-lines. They also have vivid memories of their childhood experiences. I need prompts to create the pictures, which my brain can then forge into a completed puzzle.

Many of my childhood memories are choppy. "Where are the places you've travelled to?" I've often been asked. "Which cities?" Only a few come to mind even though I've travelled extensively.

I'm now retired. It's a strange feeling. I've been going out for coffees with my mother, helping her in any way needed and seeing first hand the next stage of my life. The reality of the upcoming decade, and hopefully the one after that.

I try to think that I won't be the same

as my mother. Unfortunately, it's the inevitable outcome for all of us, if we're lucky enough to make it into the seventies and onward.

I feel that the slowing of the walking, the grunting bending over, the oohing getting up from the chair are all to prepare for my next adventure. Will I remain agile? Vital? Lucid? Who knows? Regardless, I will make the best of the circumstances afforded me and make sure there is laughter along the way. Who am I kidding? I'll be complaining all the way.

BROKEN BUM

One childhood event which remains sharp in my memory is the drama that ensued with my bestie, Iris. We were in grade five. One afternoon during lunch, Iris confided that after going to the toilet, she found a sprinkling of blood in her underwear. With her hand near the corner of her eye, Iris walked out from the toilet block and, as she came closer, I could see her eyes had welled up.

"What's the matter?"

"I don't know, but I think I'm sick. I didn't fall over or anything, but there's blood in my undies."

Imagining that she was about to bleed out, I put my arm around her shoulder and walked her to the staffroom. I couldn't wait to communicate to our teacher what had happened. I imagined an ambulance would have to be called. All students would need to return to their classes and perhaps a school assembly would be called to explain this tragedy. To my surprise, the teacher enveloped Iris's shoulders with her comforting arm, turned her head toward me as they headed into the staffroom and said, "Thankyou, I'll look after Iris. You go off and play."

I stood there in disbelief. Go off and play? I wanted to know everything, how this happened, what would happen next? Would Iris come back to school? Would she be hospitalised?

That day after school, when Mum picked me up, I explained my incredible and most concerning experience. "Mum, Iris broke her bum today. It started to bleed!"

Mum smiled.

I think the incident scarred me, as that was the last area on the body I thought would be susceptible to tragedy. I'd scraped knees, twisted arms, bumped just about every part of my body with bruises to prove it, but breaking your bum? That was out of the question.

Later, down the track, Mum explained what had happened. The period discussion we had, ended with, "All girls have to go through it, and you will too one day." Delightful. I wasn't prepared for the mood swings, cramping, bloating, breakouts and sugar cravings. These were omitted from the conversation, as were the chances of falling pregnant being a by-product of this marvellous period. I listened to many of my friends at school in year five with Iris, and then year six, Form 1 (as it was named then) getting out of sport and swimming, and some days being allowed to stay home. I used to nod, pretending to sympathise all knowingly, the symptoms and inconveniences the period brought. It wasn't until the end of Form 2 that my own period arrived. I felt left out of the pack till then, thinking I differed from everyone else. Something must have been wrong with me. It was not until much later in life that I discovered each woman has her window of fertility predestined at birth.

Fortunately, as all my groups of friends already had their periods, I was privy to their knowledge and experience, and as a newbie was ready to be welcomed into the pack at long last.

To begin with, my mother proposed the idea of using washable cloth pads. Seriously? I can't believe that was the situation then. My alternative was a cumbersome, thick pad that shifted while I moved, necessitating a garter belt to secure it. Very uncomfortable. Therefore, when one of my experienced friends suggested a tampon, I was all for it. My mother had told me tampons were not for me. A conservative mother's approach. My friend instead had a professional outlook, *Just put it in. It's like plugging a hole.* Very informative instructions. So that's what I did. Worried about potential harm due to my lack of knowledge about that region, I cautiously put in the tampon, just a little. Stuck halfway, it felt like a walnut in a nutcracker. This began hurting once I moved around and made the entire experience even more delightful. I remember being told that having a period hurts, so I just put this pain down to being a woman.

Not surprisingly, I went back to the "surfboards" as they were called. At least there was no pain involved. I discovered the trick of successful insertion was thanks to the invention of the applicator and a teacher who did not believe in missing out on swimming classes because of periods.

What I didn't expect was the phone call my mother made to her mother in Italy when my period arrived. My grandfather, who answered the call, was the first to know, followed by my grandmother who was at the receiving end of the accolades, "Patrizia is a woman now." Argh. How embarrassing! Did Mum do the same for my younger sister? I think not. Another burden of being the eldest child.

In Form Four, riding home on the school bus, relegated to the middle rows, I remember a girl talking about her escapades on the weekend with her boyfriend. She had tight, curly red hair and green eyes. She was in our class, but wasn't a close friend of mine. At age fifteen, I would have been as likely to have a boyfriend as being chosen to receive the Pulitzer Prize. The springy sixteen-year-old red-head proceeded to retell jumping off the wardrobe onto the bed scenarios, which were part of the ritual, along with her sexcapades with her nineteen-year-old boyfriend. Due to my lack of knowledge and inexperience, I believed every word. However, I couldn't understand why this was necessary. It sounded more of a circus act to me.

⇢ PREGNANCY ⇠

Having an Italian mother and grandmother meant there were no food restrictions during pregnancy. In fact, the constant reminder was to eat well. The baby has to be nourished. So, there were additions to breakfast: semolina, zabaglione and whatever else seemed rich enough to sustain a small elephant. My obstetrician wasn't overly concerned until the eighth month, when my twenty-kilo weight gain became a tad excessive. To avoid my baby being undernourished, I gave in to my milkshake cravings, something I'd never considered ordering previously. Mum explained away my food cravings by saying they reflected my body's needs. *Don't worry about the weight; breastfeeding will take care of it.*

You'd have to be incredibly naive to think an Italian mother's top priority postpartum is her weight. A three-point-eight kilo, well-nourished baby delivered, left an aftermath of fat strewn all over my well-nourished body as well. I was in no urgent hurry to return to my original weight as I was enjoying the pleasures of motherhood, until my forgotten jeans put out a call to action.

Post radiation therapy at age forty-five, hot flushes became my daily routine. At nine every night, give or take five minutes, the hot flushes started in my toes and migrated to my head. I'd disrobe and wait for the surge to pass. Mood swings galore. Weight gain, midriff expansion that takes a permanent hold regardless of how many sit-ups, crunches or leg raises I did. After a minor effort I said, *That's it, I'll keep my walking up instead.* That would have to do. Tried the aerobics, the step classes, Zumba, Barre, to no avail. It produced good calf muscles, but the flabby guts remained and stood firm, *I'm not leaving.*

Alas, there's the exhaustion; I used to brag about never needing a daytime rest. I would, in fact, mock those who did. You can't make it throughout the whole day without dooozzziiinnnggg offfff? Sorry, I just dropped off! It has become a regular thing now. I'd eat lunch and if I were at home, I'd lean back on the couch and nigh nigh. Couldn't help it. It's a "Power Nap" I insisted, considering I don't have as much power as I used to. I've turned into the Eveready bunny, only I'm at the end of its charge, where my drum is beating at a snail's pace. No energizer here.

THE DIET ROLLER COASTER

What a roller coaster I have been on over the years. Israeli diet, grapefruit diet plus the extreme soup diet that is used for patients who are to undergo surgery and need to lose weight fast. This soup is made with cabbage, pureed tomatoes, beans, and beef stock. The more you ate of this soup each day, the better. Day one was passable. Day two ended with the house reeking of cabbage, and the prospect of more for dinner made me flush the rest of the soup down the toilet and accept my cellulite. Obsessively reading the latest diet fads in magazines didn't help my weight loss efforts either.

Then there was a stint with Jenny Craig. I was also drawn to Weight Watchers shakes, in vanilla and chocolate, but they lost their appeal after a couple of weeks. The in-person meetings involved weighing ourselves, with a supportive Weight Watchers staff member inching the scale indicator to determine your weekly weight change. My eyes were glued, pleading for the scale to show some weight loss. I wanted to declare, *I all but fainted three times this week*. This was as stressful as waiting for the elusive call from a boy you liked when you were fourteen years old.

Then there were the latest diet pills. My bathroom shelf looked as if I were dealing prescription drugs. I bought and tried many tablets that promised they MAY reduce appetite only to learn that the high levels of caffeine in them kept me agitated and restless like a lion pacing its den. Adding to my list of weight control trials was the Slim Tea. Ingredients read as a list of unknown twigs and undergrowth, but it worked a charm. Unfortunately, the taste resembled soaked cardboard blended with shaved bark and dirt. An essential pre-requisite was, as long as you were home and close to the toilet, all would be well. It was due to the 'evacuation' that the weight came down. Nothing more than that. A shitty process.

A passion for fashion, that's me. My teenage years consisted of shopping for all things on trend. There were the Staggers jeans with the waistband double-buckled belt, which allowed you to inhale and exhale within an inch of your life, as the stomach was strapped in nice and tight. Absolutely a fashion item to wear on a coffee date where no ingestion of food was recommended. The short knits that matched the look also had a knitted waistband that sat just above the secured belt. These jumpers looked as if they had been washed in boiling hot water, spun on full, and finished in a hot dryer. This equated to a good sauna, massage and rub down.

On the feet were Treads. What an ingenious way of repurposing old discarded tyres. I didn't realise I was being sustainable back then. Plaited, dull toned rubber strips formed the upper part of the shoe while a solid block of rubber with grooves or treads formed the base of the sandal. Hence the name. I looked as if I'd just walked off the Beaurepaires assembly line fashion show. They were on trend, so I loved them. Corkers were another safety-hazard shoe which took over the market for a period. These platform wedges were so high I recall many cases of turned ankles, including mine. Clogs were the most uncomfortable shoe phase I'd worn and I could never understand how the Dutch managed daily life with these unforgiving, non-flexible wooden bases. Mind you, I think I have ultra-sensitive soles. One of my favourite shoes of the era was the thick heel and elevated platform "disco" shoes. When I wore these, I pictured John Travolta strutting down the street in *Saturday Night Fever*. Keeping balanced on those shoes was as a matter of "Staying Alive."

As a fashion victim, I was constantly on the hunt for trends which I could copy or create at home at a fraction of the cost. The Simplicity and Burda sewing patterns were not fulfilling my high fashion brief, and it was not until Vogue patterns brought out their designer original range that my creativity peaked. John Paul Gaultier, Issey Miyake, Mugler, and similar designers fulfilled my desire to wear something resembling original haute couture.

When the wide leg pant gained popularity in the seventies, I was first in line. As Status Quo was going to play at Festival Hall in 1978, a new pair of ocean blue, satin wide leg pants were on the kitchen table in a flash ready to be whirred together by the sewing machine. It was unfortunate that I miscalculated the thigh width by leaving only a couple of millimetre seams on either side. It was not until "Roll Over Lay Down" that my unbridled enthusiasm resulted in the seams concurrently splitting open as I stepped down from the seat I was not meant to be dancing on. Now, that was a time where I wanted to roll over, lay down and remain jammed under the seats. Being three rows down and four seats in from the enormous speakers, I not only returned home exposed but was oblivious to people's comments, as I was as deaf as a rock.

The fashionista in me struck again on another occasion during that era. To my recollection, I was in HSC and studying art as one of my beloved subjects. The painter Mondrian struck me as a geometric genius. He achieved harmonious compositions by balancing simple vertical and horizontal grid lines in primary colours. The basic black and white background was, and always has been, a monochromatic favourite of mine in both fashion and interiors. With that said, I designed my dress based on Piet Mondrian's painting. I chose a black wet-look plasticised fabric as the base of the dress and bought strips of yellow, red, blue and white plasticised fabric to contrast. The dress was a sleeveless, round neck, A-line swing style to the knee. With the geometric placement of the coloured strips, I was channelling Mondrian's *Composition with Red, Blue, and Yellow*. I felt I belonged in an episode of Mod Squad. A pair of white knee-high boots and I would have made a great background dancer for Nancy Sinatra's "These Boots are Made for Walking."

Talking about dance moves, these are another give away for some very questionable times in the evolution of music. Davy Jones from The Monkees had me side stepping from left to right with the co-ordinating swaying of the arms to match. He was my first dreamboat. Then there was the huge disco era. Forget going to the gym, the hours spent on the dancefloor equalled the perspiration and exercise of any aerobics session. I recall buying a glass of white wine, Blue Nun, and it lasting all night as we rarely returned to our table to sit. The chill of the three am breeze which hit our bodies as we left the venue made the remaining perspiration send shivers down our spine. It was worth every drop.

NOT THE SHAG

A woman's hairstyle is as much a part of her fashion statement as her clothing and accessories. My choices have included a wide range of styles. I can thank Florence Henderson from the Brady Bunch for the "Shag" haircut of the early 1970s. The layers, varying lengths and feathering, created a mullet look I thought was fabulous. I adored David Cassidy who also sported the look, so I thought emulating that hairstyle could bring me closer to the inner sanctum.

I made another interesting stylistic choice in my early twenties: a lopsided cut. On the right side of my head, I cut the hair very short, and on the left, it stayed long and layered, with a fringe swept across connecting the two sides. I convinced myself it was very fashion forward. However, forward was the last direction I wanted to face after it was done. It's very difficult trying to walk straight with your head turned permanently to the right to show the long side. I hated it. I felt like I was portraying the half-man, half-woman, Josephine Joseph, in the 1932 film, *Freaks*.

Suzi Quatro was my idol in the '70s. She represented the edgy rock chick I would have loved to have been. I could see myself hanging out with a band, wearing leather and sporting a sharp-looking shag haircut. Unfortunately, this wouldn't have gone down well at my Catholic girl's school where disapproving nuns were prevalent. They made us kneel on the floor and measure with a ruler to see that our dresses were never shorter than two inches above our knees. They would pin our dresses at the correct length, expecting us to make the adjustments by the next morning. I don't think playing in a band would have been accepted unless the Flying Nun had decided to recruit new members during a road trip. To rebel against conservatism, I remember making the brazen move to grab Dad's razor from the bathroom one afternoon and proceed to cut my fringe, making sure it looked messy, uneven and cool. Anything to be like Suzi. I inherited the nickname Spike thanks to this bold move.

I must add that I saw Suzi in concert in March 2024. At seventy-four, I admire her even more than when she was young. Forget the leather, the hairstyle, and the rock chick, this woman has achieved so much in her career, written six books, appeared on television shows, films, radio, was made Honorary Doctor of Music at Cambridge University and is now officially Doctor Quatro. She is still writing music and touring the world. At five feet tall, she is a woman exuding guts and gumption. I knew that being the first woman to play bass and become a rock and roll star was pretty impressive. She was my idol, and after seeing her again, maintains that title. Good things really do come in small packages.

What I can't understand is the ruche bum exercise pants. The ruching goes straight up the Kleiber pass, dividing the buttocks into two definable mounds. These days young women walk around in midriff tops and skin tight leggings. Not only that, but the other day a young woman was walking in front of me in this outfit. The worst part was that it was skin coloured. It looked like she was strolling down the shops nude. I know it's rude to stare, but I couldn't take my eyes off the two bowls of Jello jiggling and bobbing down the street.

Regardless of how great your derriere looks, whoever invented this fashion piece needs to do a lot of explaining.

Rolling Stone

My daughter's obsession with little stones was fascinating when she was a toddler. She used to stop and collect small pebbles from garden beds, make patterns, put them in rows and spend a great deal of time organising her stone treasures. Being a teacher, I thought this was the first sign of a Mensa child demonstrating genius. One day at my mother's house we were enjoying the spring sunshine chatting beside Mum's driveway, which had scattered red gravel in the garden bed. My little genius had her back to us and when I went to see what she was doing, there was a little finger going near her nose. *Don't put your finger in your nose* as every mother instructs, *it's dirty!* As I came closer, I saw the edge of a stone and her little finger approaching her nostril.

Noooo! Too late, the stone was already lodged a little way in. At two years of age, it's difficult to instruct children how to blow their nose, and my girl was no different. After trying multiple approaches to eject the piece of gravel, with no success, I took her to the doctor and watched as she lay motionless on the doctor's table. I put my hand over her eyes and sang "Twinkle, Twinkle Little Star" while the doctor approached the nostril with an extended pair of tweezers.

Please don't allow her to move, as this is very delicate. It can go two ways, and the second is not a good option. I recall those doctor's words clearly. I was terrified, but thankfully my baby girl could not see the fear in my eyes, as I couldn't have hidden it. The brilliance of that man's steady hand resulted in success. That was the last stone inserted anywhere.

Water droplets fell from my now adult daughter's hands onto her freshly self-tanned legs. Mentioning the slight water mark which had now appeared on her upper thigh, she said, "It doesn't matter; no one will notice." She was leaving to fly overseas to catch up with a young man she'd been friends with for years. My instinctive response was, "I hope so!"

Though surprised, she still managed a smile. It's rare we have these interchanges of laughs and innuendos. I find them fun, but my daughter prefers keeping things rather serious with me. That's fine. Laughing, being ridiculous, inappropriate, and pushing the boundaries is something I've always loved doing. I take pleasure in watching people's reactions. It's the moments when I shouldn't say something but do, that are my favourite.

My age doesn't match how young I feel. I remember when I was her age, and feel the same inside as I did then. But now I see the lines around my eyes and deeper lines on my cheeks that appear when I smile. The cleavage that has advanced in size appears crinkly when compressed. Sagging thighs and a low-slung backside — hallmarks of my 66 years — discourage me from wearing shorts. *Don't lose too much weight, otherwise you'll look gaunt and old,* I'm now advised. What caused such a dramatic shift? My continuous dieting as a teenager and woman would bring about shouts of glee when the scale dropped a kilo, or grams for that matter! Now, I'm afraid losing weight might make me look like a zombie from Michael Jackson's *Thriller*.

I wish my body and brain were more in sync. Feeling young at heart and groaning to bend over and pick up something don't quite go hand in hand.

An early sign of advancing years was my eyesight. As if on cue, my fortieth birthday heralded the start of blurriness. While extending my arm further and further away to read a magazine was tolerable, blurry street signs while driving at night was not acceptable. I started with bifocal glasses. That word seems very dated, conjuring the base of a vintage glass milk bottle worn as a monocle. The glasses used to have that visible line which divided the shortsightedness zone from the long. When I looked down too rapidly, I felt I was aboard the QE2 battling gigantic waves. Multifocal, as they are referred to now, sound far more intelligent and multi-talented. They remove the stigma of "granny glasses", those little rectangular ones which sat at the end of the nose. The zones now interface smoothly, thankfully. No need for Dramamine.

WEARING "HOLD ME INS"

I was rummaging through my wardrobe to find donations for the Red Cross appeal. It's amazing how I constantly have things to give away. I'm certain my clothes are breeding like rabbits overnight, leaving my wardrobe perpetually overflowing.

I discovered my "hold-it-in" section, as I term it, and investigated each piece. These pieces had been worn only twice, and I thought I'd best try them on to see if there was any visible sign of damage or, in fact, if they were not suitable for donation. It was incumbent on me to do the right thing. These long-lost near new items were shown the light again.

I was excited, thinking I could resurrect some of these pieces. From the back of the shelf, I fished a t-shirt style minidress that looked the perfect fit for a six-year-old. I held it up and the width barely extended from one hip bone to the next. I attempted to slip the sausage casing over my head, struggling to get one arm in, but it was near impossible. Houdini would have thought the straight-jacket escape a breeze compared to this thing. If I got caught up in this tangled mess, it may be days before I could lower my arms to make an emergency phone call. Definite donation.

Then out came the extended full brief, which holds in the side boob fadoobs. This undergarment creates a smooth, tight and curvaceous finish for any dress to simply glide over, or so the advertising claimed. As the full brief slipped on, I pulled the top up to finish under the breast line. The side fadoobs refused to be tucked in and instead kept rolling the top of the briefs down. Added to this, the weight of the breasts undulating against the stubborn fabric roll jammed it in its place. In the end, I had a pair of big undies with an added roll around my roll. Donation.

The last piece was the bra and slip in one with extended cinching fabric to below the bum line. That was *a step into* piece. Having placed both legs in, I began to wriggle, creeping the fabric up, inching my way, determined to loop those bra straps on. The problem was that the pushing up of the bum plus the gut, including the side flub, left no other option but overflowing into the bra area like a tube of toothpaste being squeezed to the top without opening the cap. Anna Nicole Smith, eat your heart out. As I valued breathing, I rolled the casing down and kicked it off, flicking it onto the discard pile.

A good start to the donations. I hope someone less sausagey will make good use of them. You're welcome.

THESE LITTLE PIGGIES STAY HIDDEN

When I walk into the manicurist and hear the water gushing into the foot massage basins, squirts of bubbles emerging into puffy scented clouds of indulgence, I sigh. My one eyebrow arches and my eyes droop with desire in anticipation of the warm pampering. Unfortunately, those basins will never see my feet. During my extensive ballet training, methylated spirits were a regular part of my routine post training. In those days metho was a way of hardening the skin to prevent aches and pains after long hours of pointe work.

I bought a pair of pointe shoes at Bloch. The salesperson told me I needed Russian ballet shoes as my ankles were very strong. It seemed to be a tremendous compliment. I was a legend in my own mind, comparing myself to the brilliant Anna Pavlova, perhaps? Let's be real. The Bolshoi Ballet was never calling me. However, thanks to the restriction of the toes in these shoes between the ages of thirteen to twenty-two, I have lovely bunions and ugly toes as a permanent reminder. I loved dancing, so there are no regrets. However, pedicures and high heels are the sacrifice one must make. My daughter is visibly irked by all feet. If I just touch her with my foot, it's a squirm and a loud *yuck*!!

On a holiday to Hong Kong, I was competing with Imelda Marcos on the number of shoes I could purchase on one trip. The choices were extensive in this gorgeous city, so I decided to try my luck in a high-end department store.

"I'd like to try these shoes in a size forty, please." A simple request.

The salesgirl, with a furrowed brow and incredulous tone, repeated my request, asking, "Size forty?"

I reassured the girl she had heard correctly. She went to the back of the store to speak with a colleague. With her back to me, I could see the colleague peer over her shoulder at me and put her hands in front of her mouth, then they both giggled.

The colleagues walked back, glanced at my shoes and said in a formal tone, "We don't stock YOUR size. Largest is size thirty-eight."

I took my Bozzo feet out of the store.

Thailand was the location of another foot-related incident several years back. I had worked up the nerve to get a massage and pedicure. My thinking was that no-one knows me there, I was in a foreign country and it wasn't my regular manicurist, so I was going to pamper my feet this once. The massage was unbelievable. I was in total bliss. The time came when the pedicurist approached. Their technique was for the client to remain lying down while their feet were attended to. Without a word, the lady took the covering sheet from my legs and applied a wet cloth to my feet. The feeling was soothing, pleasantly foreign. I lay there with my eyes closed, savouring every moment. She came to a sudden halt. I could see, from my right eye, which was barely open, another woman approaching. They were both studying my feet and discussing something. I didn't know what was being said, but most probably it was something like... *Have you ever seen such ugly feet?* or *Can you hand me a blindfold?* or *I'm not touching those!*

From that moment, all relaxation drained from my body and transformed into anxiety. I couldn't wait for the pedicurist to finish so I could squirm from the building with my feet between my legs.

ENOUGH IS ENOUGH, I'M COOKED

This morning, I woke up thinking that I'd had enough. My shoulder was aching, my neck was stiff and ribs were sore, that's another story. At five thirty a.m. the cat had started his usual routine, climbing on my back while I lay motionless, desperately wanting to keep sleeping. After a gentle nudge to the side, he began stepping over the pillow. So I swept him up in my arms and out. The bedroom door was closed. Sorry, but I needed to sleep after being awake through the early hours listening to American political discussions. Why do I do this to myself?

My brain felt like a shrivelled, desiccated prune. There is only so much I can cope with, my mother, daughter, cat and home, plus trying to reinvent myself as some semblance of a writer.

No wonder some people turn to comforting addictions. For a couple of years now I've been saying my dream is to lie on a deckchair, somewhere warm and exotic, not hot, a cocktail donning an umbrella in hand and no one I know around me.

In the meantime, bring me a party size bag of Twisties and a magnum of Prosecco. I'll make it through another day.

Perusing the aisles of the Storage King store was one of my favourite past times, inspiring creative ideas. *I could move that from a big container to a smaller one. Oooo, stackable, what a space saver!* I wanted to transfer, re-locate, assemble, stack, organise, re-position and surround myself with order. This enveloped me with a feeling of serenity. All my necklaces and jewellery are arranged in smart looking timber cutlery dividers. Colour coordinated and separated by styles. Bracelets in one section, pearls in another. Bling in its own space. Scarves are folded, with rounded edges exposed in an orderly pile. Twillies (thin neck scarves) twirled into a circle are fitted into an old tea bag separator box.

Shoes are arranged heel to toe to take up less space and be clearly seen when deciding which heel I need for a particular outfit. Handbags are aligned side by side in sizes and colour blocks. This is a household which reflects cleanliness, modernity and order. OCD? Organisation and cleanliness are an essential part of who I am. It is how I was raised. Now, with an adult daughter living at home, dishes are left in the sink, clothing piles which haven't seen a coat hanger, let alone a wardrobe in weeks, cry out for help; her bed remains unmade, dust films everywhere so thickly I can sign my name and the bathroom has more items outside the cupboards than in. Don't mention the vanity or toilet, which I dream will one day be self-cleaning.

After years of picking up, putting away, cleaning, sorting, tidying, I'd hoped that I would have a helper in my one and only child. It seems old habits are hard to break. To keep my sanity and anxiety at bay, I am still the picker upper, the put-away-er, the sorter, the cleaner, and the tidier. It is my issue, I know. OCD- Occasional Crisis Diverter or Over-loaded Crazy Dame. Serenity now!

MEMORIES

When you are about to leave the house for a holiday a peculiar panic descends. Have I got everything? The various adapters, phone chargers, EarPods, iPad, Apple Watch, power pack. That's the electronics done. Then there are the converters, plugs, and extras in case they don't fit (I've been caught out several times.) Have I covered all possible seasonal changes in clothing? Shoe string straps, short sleeve, three quarter sleeve, light-weight long sleeve and thicker long sleeve. Full length pants, narrow leg and a wide leg option. A skirt, a jacket and a couple of dresses. Shoes need to cover a range of options as well. Runners and a sneaker or two, a ballet flat, a heel (however, now it's a demi or block heel for comfort).

Thinking through each step has become part of the day-to-day routine. It's like someone coming in and patting me down before I leave the house. Do I have my spare shopping bag, wallet, keys, phone? How many times have I walked out the door and realised once at the car that my phone isn't there to plug into the charger? Then it's back up the stairs, in search of where it was left. Never in an obvious place. Sometimes it's in a cupboard, left as I was contemplating the choice of bag or shoe. Perhaps under the pile of clothes I'd thrown on top of it in a rush? It doesn't help that I leave my phone on silent to not disturb anyone, especially as I've been caught out in the middle of the night when the ding of the spam texts come in. *Your MyGov account has a message for you.* At 3 am? I don't think so. The eye rolls I receive from my daughter when I walk back in. *You've forgotten your phone again?*

Mind you, the phone is everything. It's such a scary feeling to think it's lost. All your life is exposed. Details only privy to you. I wish the Find my Phone app would just go out and find my phone. The memory loss that occurs as you age may be normal but difficult to get used to. It's like walking on a tightrope. You could fall either way. It's the balancing pole which needs to get longer to keep everything in equilibrium.

SILENCE

Sometimes I sit in silence. Complete silence. I listen to the quiet and find solace in it, bringing mindfulness to the moment. After a day filled with television news reports, podcasts, YouTube videos, Instagram posts, TikTok reels, bustling supermarkets, crowded shopping centres, hectic cafes, bumper to bumper traffic, requests for dinner, demanding cat, texting mother, silence is all I dream of. "Serenity now!" as Seinfeld character Frank Costanza would say. My mantra, *Serenity; bring it on.*

THE AGING PARENT- THE ELDERLY STAGE

It would seem the death of your parents marks the end of your childhood. Reaching full adulthood and independence hinges on that. Since my father's passing almost ten years ago, I have had the primary responsibility for my mother. My father was the main decision maker, the financial administrator and protector. My mother's role was looking after her two girls and the home. My father was a successful man and I admire and appreciate all he did for us. However, this left my mother very dependent on him, a generational curse affecting many women. The experience of dealing with my mother since his death has been all-consuming. Her newfound autonomy has left me completely bewildered.

Frequently, when discussing alternative options for a financial transaction, she gave me a blunt, *Do as I tell you*. It left me speechless, catching me by surprise, until I reminded Mum there was no need to speak to me that way. I felt as if I'd returned to my ten-year-old self and was being reprimanded for not cleaning my room. I felt strange telling Mum how I felt, as normally I would keep things to myself. I was comforted by my best friend's tale of when she *threw a pound of butter at Mum one day, in pure frustration at her rudeness towards me.* She regretted it, but told me her action had completely changed the dynamic. Interesting.

I have also observed how self-centred one becomes when entering old age, focusing on one's own needs as a priority. Having coffee together with the same dearest girlfriend and Mum, I stepped away for a bathroom break, when quite adamantly Mum told my friend *It's all about me now. I'm the most important one in the family.* My friend relayed this bold statement to me that evening and told me all she could do was nod.

While I feel empathy towards how difficult growing old can be, I'd like to remind my mother how lucky you are to be here, in relatively good health, considering your body has been chugging along for close to ninety-one years, is pretty remarkable. Considering you've had a brilliant run with no prior bone breakages, cancer diagnosis, dementia outlook or any other major diseases is a blessing and something to be mindful of and grateful for. To have your family close to you and doing everything they can to please you and continue to make life as easy for you as it can be, is a fortunate place to be.

You just have to step back and take a moment to appreciate your life, in whatever circumstances you may find yourself.

My mother's behaviour has been a window into my future and now I understand how difficult it is to be present every day for an elderly parent. You do it with love. However, when it's my turn, I will book myself into a facility and take the responsibility away from my daughter.

If you know of a facility that has a pool, bar and dancefloor, please forward me the link.

THE SAHARA OF SKIN

Nurturing anything to grow on my skin would resemble trying to grow flowers on Mars or the Sahara. There is no chance this barren, parched land can sustain, let alone provide the infrastructure and resources, to support growth. The once thriving landscape, maintained moisture, firmness and elasticity for years. Now the sandpapery, dry and wrinkled epidermis is constantly demanding moisturiser. The thicker, the better. I would love to be immersed in a tub filled with coconut oil, petroleum jelly, aloe vera and honey. Upon exiting, I'd either stick the landing or skid straight out of the bathroom.

CESSATION OF REGISTRATION

Because of the significant time and energy commitment required for my mother's care, I cancelled my teacher's registration. This was a difficult tab to press. But I did it. I'm retired, it's official. Like a vasectomy, this can be undone, but it's not a simple process. It involves considerable effort, pain, and commitment.

My career brought me joy, happiness, and fulfillment. Among my most treasured memories is kneeling down to console a distraught three-year-old, only to receive an unforeseen, wet, snotty sneeze straight to my face. This vocation comes with rewards. I smiled, after scrubbing my face.

A sweet year one student struggled to show her feelings, so each day after school, I'd receive a powerful whack in the stomach as I stood farewelling the children at the exit door. When discussing this with the parents, they described her actions as a way of showing affection. I smiled. One Monday morning, my six-year-old year one student arrived at school sporting a shiny silver stud earring, which his dad pridefully declared was his birthday gift. I grinned. Interacting with a selective mute in my four-year-old kindergarten class presented challenges. I spent a year winning him over, gently building his trust and confidence. It wasn't until the last term of the year that I had to ask him to quieten down. I felt a great sense of personal satisfaction. What a beautiful boy. Thinking about him still brings a smile to my face, and I hope he's found happiness and contentment in his life.

There's nothing more rewarding than the times when a child considers you as someone special. An eight-year-old girl in my year three class moved me deeply. She was five when her mother passed away from cancer, and her father raised her from that point. As we said goodbye at the end of the year, she rushed towards me, gave me a big hug, and whispered, "I don't want you to leave. I want you to be my mother."

This brought not only a smile, but also tears.

I hope that my work with the many special needs children in my classes has positively impacted their school experiences. How lucky was I?

How Many Vitamins Can One Buy?

My enthusiasm outweighs my dedication when it comes to vitamin supplements. If I read an article or see an ad on television that makes me think this vitamin or supplement is going to help with my anxiety or gut health or sleeplessness or joint pain or hair loss or energy levels, I'm off to the pharmacy or supermarket to buy yet another pill. This is where my enthusiasm ends. The new container takes its place among the double-decker pile of existing little helpers. They are like soldiers lined up, waiting to be called to duty.

There are small rubbery jelly pills, round chalky ones and horse tablets big enough to make you consider why you're taking your life in your own hands each time you try to swallow one. My problem is I'm not consistent in taking them and the number of pills I have keeps growing. If I were to take one of each as recommended daily, you'd be hearing me coming from afar, rattling like a bag of MnMs.

TIME TO STOP MAKING RESOLUTIONS

The new year is around the corner. With it comes excitement, anticipation and the yearly resolutions I make. At the end of each three hundred and sixty-five days, the enthusiasm and elation that once came with the year ahead now vanishes. Pre-Christmas celebrations are usually capped off with the statement *I'm sure next year will be great. This is your year. I can feel it, exciting times ahead!* While I appreciate the kind words of encouragement and wisdom espoused by my friends, I reflect and think that as I didn't achieve what I set out to achieve last year, we may as well be realistic. What's the point of setting myself up for failure? The storage cage in the garage I intended to clean out has not been opened. I think about selling the goods instead. Then I realise this means dealing with social media, photographing, communicating, bargaining, posting, meeting, refunding and everything else. I give up. It's not for me.

Then there's the traditional *I need to lose at least two kilos this year*, which amounts to a gain of at least three instead. I often think about fat loss. Where does it go? It was there two weeks ago, and the scales now tell me I've lost a kilo. I have this image of a fat cloud surrounding you and dissipating as you walk along the street.

Next year, I need to sort through the photos I have on my phone. Every time I need to show someone a photo, it exasperates me to no end. *Hang on, it's here somewhere. What year was it? Let me see if I can use the search bar. Why have I got a photo of a chair leg?* Scrolling and scrolling, to no avail. If I were to have printed each photo from the phone as was the way of the olden days, with nearly 6000 photos and 400 videos, I'd need to build an extra room just to house the photo albums. I'd also need to catalogue them according to year, genre and theme. Please, no. Daunting task, so I've clicked delete on a few photos and that's it. But the number continues to grow.

Being a practical, sensible and reasonable person, I have decided from now on no more new year resolutions will take place, photos can and will accumulate. Let's face it, who looks at a photo from the day you first bought your iPhone? The storage cage will be decluttered once it becomes full enough that the goods protrude through the chicken wire like sausage through a sieve, and the kilos will come off once I admit that Twisties and wine are not staple dietary foods.

STOP BEING ANXIOUS

Recently my ninety-year-old mother said, while we were enjoying a decaf coffee, *You need to let things go. Stop being anxious.* Coming from a mother who has always had acute anxiety, perfectionism and self-inflicted stress as part of her personality, it's ironic how she identifies my anxiety.

Anxiety is a difficult beast to domesticate. You can't just switch it off, and unless you are in a comatose state because of medications, you don't just get up in the morning thinking, *Ahh, can't wait to see what I can be anxious about today.* Mum explained that she had been very clear to her doctor many years ago, after being told to eliminate stress and anxiety from her daily life, that it would only ever be achievable when she was dead. Therefore, my response to her was; *You see? I'm the same as you. Anxiety is passed down. It is a shared genetic vulnerability.*

I got it, along with most of the past family's health issues. Someone had to carry it on. Might as well be me. I don't want to sound like a martyr, but I'm honest about it. The other part of my vulnerable personality is that I'm hopeless when dealing with people or animals who are suffering. I become this droning *awwwww* sounding woman.

One method of easing my anxiety has been to reduce caffeine and replacing it with decaffeinated coffee has made a significant difference. I can better cope with the cat scratching the living daylights out of the corners of my boucle couch, pulling all threads from my grey linen fabric bedhead, kicking kitty litter to all corners of the bathroom, having a suitcase opened and still packed for three weeks in the living room after my daughter's return from an overseas holiday, finding dishes left in the sink, kitchen bench and coffee table and dust accumulating where it previously never stood a chance.

I'd better stop now. Time for a decaf.

ANY EXCUSE

One night when my daughter returned home from work, I suggested we move our planned trip to Seoul forward from March to early December and leave in three weeks. We had a window of opportunity. The excitement started setting in. Perfect time to see the Christmas decorations and pick up a few extra gifts. We could really get into the festive mood. Let's get out the bubbles and celebrate.

These days I'm finding many things to celebrate. That in itself is enough to bring out the Prosecco. The cat turns one. Pop! I got through the day without hearing negativity. Pop! My stomach is not as puffy today. Pop! Pop! Today I might have a break from carting heavy bags from the supermarket and cook whatever drops out of the pantry. Prosecco time! The dusting AND the washing were completed in one day. Fizz time. It's Friday again. Open the bottle. Not another month coming up like this past one? Better open two bottles.

Is this as good as it gets? Bring me the

wine vat. How easily one sips, I mean slips.

DON'T BE NOSEY

In my 66 years I have yet to encounter a woman who possesses complete confidence in her appearance. It's a shame really, but I guess that is who we are as women. This is a generalisation.

All it took was one evening at a nightclub in my 20s. A comment made by a friend of a friend that stayed with me all my life. *Your nose is quite big, isn't it?* Seven words. From that day on, I became self-conscious of my nose. I felt like saying to that person, *Okay, but who are you comparing my nose to? Jimmy Durante? Are you a surgeon specialising in rhinoplasty? What qualifies you to tell me my nose is quite big, apart from your good eyesight?* I feel it is quite in proportion to the rest of my face. My theory is that noses usually are. Mind you, I envy those women who have cute, petite noses as much as I envy those who have delicate straight toes manicured exquisitely and exposed for all to see.

In conclusion, his off-hand remark taught me to be careful with the comments I make. Of course, if you wish to offend someone, then that's your prerogative, but what you say can stick. It affected me much more back then. Another great bonus of aging is that I don't care as much these days.

Some days when I look in the mirror, I remember those words, and smile. This proboscis has served me well and I have no complaints. I'll just work on making my hairstyle bigger, to balance it out. I'll be channelling Effie.

SO CLOSE

At sixty-six, I relish the control I have over my life. Hang on a moment, my daughter has moved back home with me, which I love, though I'm sure she has a different perspective. I have a cat who needs me and my ninety-year-old mother depends on me. Freedom is not there quite yet.

After messages of *What are we having for dinner tonight* and *have you bought the cat food today*? Then the nine text messages from Mum. *Did I tell you about Lily? She has a terrible shake now. Poor thing, she can't eat properly.* Another text. *I can't hear the sound of the messages coming in. How come another message is coming in?* Then *Did you note the date for the podiatrist?*

The freedom of being sixty-six is going to take a bit of time to realise itself. I can wait.

Joys of Aging

As you get older, your focus moves towards issues and ailments. My mother says that when she and her friends, all in their eighties, get together for coffee, their principal topic is what's been going wrong in their lives that week. If you have had nothing drop off, become infected, seriously hurting, inflamed, throbbing or aching, you might as well skip lunch otherwise you'd have to resort to last week's ailment, and they will have heard it already. *Oh that*, you'll hear, *we heard about your leg last week. Now listen to this. Do you know what the doctor told me this week?* The joys of aging.

IT'S A BUM MOVE

I'm cranky at people who wear their backpacks on a plane as they meander up the aisle only to discover their seat is opposite mine. There is always a turn involved and a near decapitation as the backpack clunks me on the head. It's as bad as the people who walk facing away from the movie screen as they side step across to their seats. I always seem to be the recipient of a bum thumping there as well.

Recently I had a discussion reflecting on whether you should walk facing away or towards the people seated in a theatre? Think about it. I've seen both. Perhaps there should be a regulations list in the foyer of all theatres:

PLEASE ADHERE TO THE FOLLOWING RULES

Face the screen as you move across to your seat.

Assure that bathroom stops have been made prior to the commencement of the show.

Any packaged items should be opened prior to entering the theatre.

Extra tall people only permitted to use aisle or back row seating.

Remove your hat in the theatre, regardless of the state of your hair. Consider dry shampoo in the future.

Anyone who wishes to conduct continuous conversations or commentary will be promptly removed.

CAROUSEL COURTESY

At the airport carousel, I courteously stand back to allow people to view their bags, however, undoubtedly there is always someone who comes and stands right in front of me, blocking my view of the bags completely. Do some people not understand personal space? Courtesy? Politeness? How would they like it if I should then step straight in front of them and do the hand (body) slap game all the way to the front.

⁘ TOILET PAPER ⁘

What boils my oil is finding myself in a cubicle which has cheap toilet paper as thin as a single layer of tissue paper or as delicate as a butterfly's wing. Rolling that paper wheel round and round until I finally grab any segment, the challenge is to obtain a few squares, only to find that the paper has a width of half a centimetre, as it's already been mauled by other desperate women in the same position. This string of tissue keeps breaking as I continue to cautiously turn it as if I am performing delicate surgery. At the end of this process, I'm left with a handful of shredded bits which are as useful as trying to wipe up a spill with plastic film.

ROAD RULES I'M ANNOYED AT

1. Drivers who pull up beside you on the left at a red light, then proceed to leave half their tyres on the pavement to speed ahead and end up behind another line of cars. Congratulations, you've made it one car closer to your designated destination.
2. Drivers who pull out in front of you and then are on a go slow once they're on the main road. It's even worse when I'm alone on the road and they still pull out in front of me. Just couldn't wait that extra three seconds for me to pass. I wish I had Inspector Gadget's 1982 car with its built-in punching glove and extendable arm. If anyone tries to block me, they'll get a good walloping! But oh yes, it's much better to make me brake, slow down and allow you inconsiderate dimwit to take the pole position.

THE FACETIME CALL

Is there anything more annoying than being in a cafe enjoying a moment of peace and being forced to listen to some stranger's conversation over FaceTime at a decibel level loud enough to be heard above a group of jackhammers?

THE CHOCOLATE CUPCAKE

At the restaurant table in front of me, a family enters and the child's seating preference becomes a five-minute topic of conversation. *Would you like to sit near Grandma? What about near Mummy? Do you want to sit on the cushion?* I'm thinking, who's the adult here? Just decide and tell the child where to sit. I'm sure he will be just fine.

On this day, Mum, Grandma and four-year-old arrive at a cafe at brunch time. Then Mum asks twenty questions about what he'd like to eat. *Do you want eggs? How about toast? Orange juice?* The little boy giggles, looks under the table and flicks Grandma's hand away as she tries to have him focus on Mum's questions. He was as interested as a sloth in a fifty-meter dash.

Mum ordered. I was intrigued to see what she had decided after the Spanish inquisition.

Ten minutes later, Grandma receives a fluffy omelette, Mum a generous lamb salad Turkish roll, and the boy had a large plate with fruit and yogurt placed in front of him. He looked at it and then stood up on the bench behind the table, no interest in the food whatsoever. In the next second came a chocolate cupcake. Mum points to the fruit and yogurt, gesticulating that he needs to eat that as a priority. Again, all instructions are ignored, and he goes straight for the cupcake. So much so that at one point he bends his face forward and, without using his hands, takes a huge mouthful. Mum keeps pointing and harping at the fruit and manages to jab one piece of banana into his mouth.

Honestly, I don't understand.

If you wanted your child to eat a healthy bowl of fruit and yogurt, why on earth did you order the cupcake? Did you really expect your child to eat through this adult sized portion and then settle quietly to enjoy a cupcake? It was tortuous to watch the badgering. Poor boy.

NOT BY THE HAIR ON MY CHINNY CHIN CHIN

The hairy upper lip has always been a problematic issue for many women. As a young woman, I was told several theories to control the mo. Don't wax as the hair comes in thicker. That was a seriously scary notion. I could see myself strip off the first lot and wake up the next morning with a Tom Selleck 'tash in full bloom.

Then there was the bleaching period. Unfortunately, the stench caused by the bleach was problematic as it stunk up the entire bathroom, and the yellowish colour ended up looking as if I had a parched grassland under my nose.

Last resort was plucking. That was a tear jerker, as the hairs closest to the base of the nose, the philtrum, were painful to remove. I returned to my original fear and thought I'd best let destiny prevail and wax. I was surprised that the hair did not grow thicker, but it did toughen up. The newbie hairs declared that if I were going to keep pulling them out, I was going to have to put up with prickles. At my age, it's not as great an issue as it was then. The thought of coming across an unexpected evening or date when I might end up kissing someone, and I hadn't mowed the lawn, was enough to plaster Band-Aids all over the upper lip claiming I'd mistakenly scalded my lips on a bowl of boiling hot soup at lunch. Anything was better than a young man caressing your face only to pull back, yelling, *OUCH!*

Now the bigger issue is chin hair. I'm sure the number of chin hairs increases yearly. As candles are a reminder of each birthday, so are the number of chin and lip hairs. I'd surely count sixty-six of the annoying things.

Toddlers with Mobiles

One warm sunny day, I was taking Mum on an outing. As I waited for her to emerge from the house, a young father came pushing a pram along the footpath. As he passed, I spotted the toddler's feet popping out. My thoughts were, how lovely, a young father walking along allowing some valuable time for his child to rest among the tweeting of the birds and soft breeze. As he crossed the road and headed past me, I noticed the toddler was not resting. Was he enjoying the magnificent day? No. The top of the pram was halfway down, creating a dark, gloomy, cave-like environment and in front was a mobile phone, propped up with the child transfixed to the moving video.

An identical situation happened this morning as I was having coffee. I noted a mum and dad chatting while their two or three-year-old was sitting beside them with eyes glued to the phone screen. The child was to the left of the couple as they faced each other in deep conversation. He didn't move but remained transfixed to the screen and took a knife and began putting that into his mouth while still not diverting his eyes from the program he was watching. Mum and Dad didn't glance at him until it was time to leave.

I guess it's the teacher in me, but I often wonder about the generation coming up now. Why do they have to be constantly distracted, dependent on entertainment props. Whatever happened to communication, observation, participation and just plain immersion in life? It's all instant gratification and a quick turnaround these days. When my daughter was young, my handbag always had a notebook, pencils, a couple of mini books and packets of stickers. They only came out when we were in cafes or restaurants, so they remained a novelty. Of course, I had to invest more time into reading or writing with her, but the reward in seeing her creativity develop was immeasurable. Today she works in the creative arts.

I'm not saying that I was the ideal parent. This is far from the truth. We all make mistakes and I have made many, but I can never say that I didn't take part in her development as a child. Being present as a parent is difficult, tiring, trying, time consuming and never ending but I wouldn't have changed it for the world.

Thank goodness mobile phones were not around then. I would like to challenge parents to return to the non-device days. For at least the first couple of formative years of their child's life. The devices will become part of everyday life soon enough. Just take the time to allow your children to observe the world, question the world and develop patience by not surrendering to their every whim by providing distracting entertainment.

⩵ ANNOYANCES, GRIEVANCES AND APPRECIATIONS ⩵

Miscarriages are a tragedy. I experienced three in one year, and there are no words to describe the loss. I desperately wanted a sibling for my daughter, but this wasn't to be. Bereavement differs for everyone. I had named each child from the moment the pregnancy was confirmed. Happy news. A miracle, a joy and a blessing for women who want a child.

Each loss was the loss of all I dreamed that child could be.

I thank my girth, my flab and my wrinkles for all they have given me. If it weren't for this body of mine, faults, fault lines, crevices and curves, my beautiful girl wouldn't be with me. Thanks, you gorgeous piece of woman.

And her too.

Humidity Hair and Maintenance

The whole hair maintenance is never ending. I have some girlfriends who have embraced the grey and achieved peace through accepting their destiny. Plus, they're saving a ton of money. Then I have another dearest friend whose mantra is hair and nails. *That is something I'll never compromise on.*

Good on them all. For me? I'm not at the grey hair acceptance stage. As far as I can see, I have a smattering of greys around the perimeter so it would look like a bad regrowth situation if I left that unattended for too long. I did progress from a darker tint to a lighter one over the last couple of years. It was a dramatic change from the very blonde I had worn for many years. My daughter suggested, *Go darker Mum, it makes you look younger*. How could I not want to look a tad younger? I asked, *How many months will it shave off my age? Two? Three?* I gave it a go and liked it. My view on change has always been, bring it on. I have progressively lightened my hair colour until I reached a semblance of my natural light brown.

Throughout my life, my hair has been cared for with enough shampoos, conditioners, volumizing sprays, nourishing creams, treatments, powders, dry moisturising oils and hair perfumes to fill a Chemist Warehouse. Let's not contemplate trying to add up the cost of this, including hairdressing appointments, top of the line blow dryers and brushes, clips, headbands and hair accessories.

I could have made a downpayment on a house instead. Maintenance is costly, not only in dollars, but hours. I realise I'm not a grey embracer, yet I'm not an obsessed hair aficionado anymore. While my appearance is important to me, I'm now prepared to be seen with humidity hair. I refuse to spend any time flattening with serums and sprays, only to walk out the door and within minutes looking like an electrified lion's mane. No point putting the remaining precious hairs through torture when they have little chance against the elements. One big upsweep and twist of the hair secured with a claw clip and off I go. No-one needs to know that once upon a time I would never have been seen in public wearing this unkempt excuse for a hairdo. Now I embrace the humidity and my confidence.

The worst part of our Melbourne summers are the frequently humid days. I have bought anti-frizz hair balm, anti-frizz hair spray, anti-frizz anything else I can find. I've looked up YouTube clips on minimising frizz but everything has come to nought. My hair is less a hairstyle as it is an "atmospheric condition". It has more volume than my bank account. Normally I blow dry it flat with a kick at the shoulder. On these humid days, along with my face and neck dripping with perspiration, the hair cannot be left to its own devices. To a passerby, my hair is saying, *I don't give a s**t, I've not been washed or styled in months!*

My only resort is to pull it back so I resemble a bowling ball with glasses. However, given the alternative, I feel this is a reasonable compromise. If the make-up I apply in the morning would stay on, that would give me the appearance of a woman who has made an attempt to comply with social standards. Seeing that the perspiration creates a landslide of foundation, eyeshadow and mascara, I am better off applying a smear of lipstick and keeping it simple.

During our summer, a once high heeled, slim-fitting dress wearer, hair and makeup proud woman, has evolved into a tent wearing, sneaker, lick of lipstick with no visible hair creature who should never stray from air-conditioning. I need an industrial cooler strapped on me twenty-four seven.

NAILED IT

Embracing my humidity hair has allowed me to embrace another part of my body's lack of tip-top maintenance. The ten little nails on my hands. I refer to these only, the nails on the toes are not included for, as you may recall from a previous chapter, my toes are for my eyes only, within reason of course.

The invention of SNS and Shellac or gel, as its often known, was a great idea. The one thing I detest is chipped nail polish. What is the point of dressing beautifully, accessorising magnificently, only to see chipped nails bringing a cup of coffee to the mouth? Or a champagne to the lips? It's like seeing a man bend over only to spot the crack. Not a good look.

At last, I found a solution to having to reapply nail polish every few days, as a chip would undoubtedly always occur.

Manicure.

Off I went again, soaking the nails in acetone or wrapping them in little foil tips, scraping the living daylights out of them as the old SNS nail polish was removed or drilled as if boring for oil, as the machine takes off the polish, layer by layer. This seemed a better option than putting up with chipped nails. The manicure was the answer to my chip obsession, (hot chips coming in at a close second).

However, with a renewed perspective on the manicure and with acceptance of my humidity hair, perfectly manicured hands didn't seem an obsessive necessity any more. A couple of weeks later, I returned to the nail salon and the Shellac polish was removed. I felt comfortable embracing bare nails, freeing them from encumbrances, allowing them to breathe again. Seeing my nails au naturel gave me a sense of freedom. Another step in acceptance. I felt empowered. Bare, but liberated.

I'm now considering increasing my use of long beaded necklaces, changing my Prada eyeglasses for rimless granny ones, dressing in loose clothing, (which suits me so well) wearing moccasins, (can't do barefoot) and a fringed handbag. I'll totally embrace the freedom look. Peace man!

Ozempic seems to be everywhere. The housewives I watch during my brain freezing moments are all looking fabulous. Many are open about using the medication and there are those that aren't. I find it hard to believe that doing some exercise is the reason they dropped a third of their body weight before the start of the next season. From experience, I know how difficult it is to budge one kilo, let alone ten or more. You'd have to be running a marathon each week to reach that goal in a couple of months. I must admit I looked into Ozempic out of curiosity. Unfortunately, I go straight to the side effects and that makes me think, perhaps it's not for me.

SINGLE PARENTS

An enormous round of applause to all the single parents out there. It is a demanding yet rewarding journey, filled with challenges and opportunities, sadness and joy. During my cancer diagnosis and treatment many years ago, my husband left the family home. This traumatic time left my five-year-old daughter and me having to negotiate a new life as I battled cancer alone. It was hard to find a balance between looking after myself as well as my child. She was a sweet girl with a head full of blonde curls, deep brown eyes; timid, except with her mother.

During my early parenting years, "controlled crying" was becoming popular, as was the "time out" theory. Leaving a small child to soothe themselves is impossible without the help of a parent. That was my experience. Hearing the deep state of distress which develops after a prolonged period of the baby crying is too painful to bear. I was unsuccessful with this process and felt I was a weak mother for giving in to the cries.

Today I'd love to sit down with the child psychologist or whoever decided this was a better option and ask them why?

The "time out" theory was a reasonable option, I thought. So I decided I would implement this strategy every time my daughter defied me. The first time I used it was when she was three and had misbehaved. *Go to your room and wait for me to come and get you.* Our bedrooms were at opposite ends of an upstairs corridor. I took my mischievous little girl and delivered her into her room and upon closing the door, instructed her to stay there until I came to get her. *From now on, if you do that again, you'll have to go to time out.*

I felt empowered and proud I was practising a proven theory. I closed the door and as I was halfway up the corridor, I heard the creak of her door and footsteps marching straight behind me. I turned around and led her back into her room in one quick motion. Repeat the process and guess what? The same result. The door creaked open and out she came. I tried twice more and thought, where is the instruction manual on what to do now? It's against the law to lock her in her room, so what now? The defiance that my toddler showed me at three years of age should have alerted me to the strong-minded, independent young woman I was going to experience later in life. When I re-tell my daughter this story, she laughs and proudly claims, *See? I've always done what I think is right!* And she has.

A transition of power occurs when your child confides in you and then ends the conversation by saying, *I didn't ask for your opinion.* It makes you reflect on the contribution that is required. *I just wanted to talk about it.* This was the moment I needed to realise that she didn't want my opinion, or ask for it, so why was I giving it? As a parent, and in my case a teacher as well, I was constantly looking to resolve problems, come up with alternative solutions, pose questions, and offer advice. As my daughter grew, the reliance she had on me began waning, and rightly so. Unfortunately, there is no "advice needed" button that is easy to switch off. It keeps jamming and wanting to give opinions.

I have made a concerted effort and deliberately tell myself, *Just listen! Shut-up!* There has been an improvement in my view and probably in my view only. I dare not ask her.

Seeing that I was an epic failure at controlled crying and time out, I'm hoping I will excel in listening and lots of nodding, hoping the magic words will be uttered one day, *What do YOU think, Mum?*

The dilemma is not "cognitively" becoming old but knowing that I am older. There is a fine line between acting, feeling and being sixty-six. Sixty-seven is around the corner and the number seventy I'd rather not consider just at the moment.

I have had many conversations with my dearest friend about this subject. Her philosophy is, "You need to do as you want now as you never know what will happen."

"I get that," I say, "but I'm not sure if I need to keep doing what I'm doing or just leave everyone to their own devices?"

In saying that I'm talking about looking after my mother and helping my daughter. Years ago, I thought both would be independent and I would have my time. But, in reality, my daughter is independent in her thinking, dreams and desires, but the reality of the financial burdens of today's life have been prohibitive when trying to create an independent home for herself. My mother, on the other hand, expresses every desire and determination to remain independent while not seeing the pressures her choices have created and how they have affected her family. At the same time, I understand her reluctance to let any independence go. However, for the safety of herself and others, I wish things were different.

Growing older is not always fun and I now understand what lies ahead. However, the approach you take is very important. How your decisions will affect others is paramount. I am optimistic about the future and so continue to toss up the question: should I save or should I spend?

TODAY THERE ARE TOO MANY CHOICES

Why has life become so complicated? Shopping is fun when you are choosing a new pair of shoes or a pair of earrings, something that will give you joy when you step out in the world. What doesn't give me joy is standing in front of the toothpaste aisle, having to decide which toothpaste I need to choose. I need to acknowledge I'll never get back the next five minutes of my life.

Do I want to brighten my teeth? At this age it's probably a good choice, but then I have to choose between a dearer or cheaper alternative. Does paying more give me brighter teeth? I don't want a fluorescent finish, so if I come into contact with a neon light, all you'll see is a set of teeth coming towards you. Looking across the shelves there are tartar control, (which sounds rather offensive as if there is green, hairy mould that grows daily on teeth), cavity control, sensitive, whitening sensitive, all day sensitive, gum care, antibacterial, multi-protection, whitening with hydrogen peroxide (that should go straight to your hair I thought as ingesting could have lethal consequences). The plethora of products fill me with choice overload.

Do I protect my gums and sacrifice the cavities? Do I whiten my teeth and risk that my gums will recede? Do I use total day control or be content with a few happy hours? Consumerist anxieties thrive in the toothpaste aisle, where the pressure to make the 'right' choice transforms a basic hygiene routine into a hair pulling experience. As they know these options exist in the market, why can't they combine them into one tube? A whitening, cavity and tartar protecting, sensitive, antibacterial all day multi-protection toothpaste... with a touch of mint. Sold!

And let's not get started on shampoos.

I Need to Give a Shout Out to Seoul

It's my third time visiting Seoul. Thanks to my daughter's passion for all things Korean, what started as a sceptical argument regarding what on earth she saw in this country, I have joined her in understanding the appeal.

It feels so foreign (pun intended) to be surrounded by respectful people, people who wait in systematic lines to board a train. Once on board, pushing and loud voices on phones are frowned upon. Everyone sits silently with eyes focused on their devices. You can eat off the spotless floor in every hygienic carriage. I have often witnessed an employee walking through each carriage, broom in hand, picking up an occasional stray piece of paper. The coffee culture is also different as coffee shops, bakeries and a mix of both are offered every few metres. When I look in, they all seem to thrive, with people sitting around on their devices or engaged in conversation.

What I found wonderful is that, if I need to use the bathroom throughout my coffee sojourn, there is no need to pack everything up and drag it to the bathroom, I can leave everything on the table, phone, wallet and all. You can be assured that nobody would ever dream of touching your things. What an extraordinary concept. It's a country that made it possible for me to feel at ease when my daughter lived and worked there. As a single young woman on her own, I breathed a sigh of relief knowing that assaults, robberies and gun violence are not tolerated. My respect for this culture is high. Of course, it is not perfect, as no country is, but kudos to respect, integrity, honesty and manners as being the "soul" of Seoul, Korea.

THE "OLOGIST"

There are bad "ologists" and good "ologists". I don't want a call from an oncologist, neurologist, cardiologist or haematologist, but a visit to a mixologist, followed by a sexologist (yes, it's a scrabble word worth 18 points) plus a gemmologist would work well for me.

If the cosmetologist and meteorologist work together, there could be a seismologist who may predict an earth-shattering future partnership on the cards.

Triple Whammy

One of my favourite foods in this world is cheese. I adore most kinds of cheese. They are delicious, delectable, but detrimental. I'm lactose intolerant. A cruel twist of fate. Being Italian, garlic and onion are also a staple part of the cuisine. But as I'm also fructose intolerant, it's a NO to onion and garlic. Oh well, you say, at least as an Italian you can enjoy warm, crusty bread. Sorry, I'll throw in the wheat intolerance and I have the triple whammy.

I just want a garlic cheesy pizza, please. Is that too much to ask?!

IS IT OKAY TO BE DECISIVE?

I often ask myself this question. I've been told many times by friends, *You always get things done straight away, I couldn't do that*, or, *I take ages to decide what to do*, and *You should have been the head of a company.* Seriously? I couldn't think of anything worse than having to deal with people's emotions in order to make them feel good. Leadership is not what I consider a joyous experience, even though I've taken on that role.

I was director of an Early Learning Centre for a couple of years and during my tenure, the centre was inspected by the education department. This is a standard practice for the industry and is a serious challenge to ensure that the quality standards and policies are met and maintained by the staff. The pressure is great in the lead up to this process and it is usually unannounced, so that authenticity prevails.

I successfully delegated tasks that week, ensuring mission success despite the looming deadline. I asked a temporary staff member, who was a friend of mine, to collect some reams of copy paper from across the road at the primary school. Perhaps I didn't ask in the gentlest way, perhaps I should have smiled more, perhaps I should have walked her to the door. Perhaps I was too decisive. Whatever it was, that request was thrown back in my face days later. "You didn't ask me nicely," was the reason I had been given the cold shoulder for the following days.

In the moment's whirlwind, I was unaware of my actions. *Is everything alright? You seem upset?*

I could not believe that a friend of mine could not think past herself for one moment and put herself in my shoes. After many apologies from my end, our friendship ended in tatters. Never to be renewed. Even coming across her in the school grounds resulted in uncomfortable silence. I'm very diplomatic and professional in the workplace. I wish others would respect that and find it in themselves to move on for the benefit of an harmonious workplace.

Conscious acknowledgement in the moment isn't typical for me. In a café in Seoul, decaf Americano in hand, I just sat. How often do I just sit and be? Rarely. My brain is normally clogged with thoughts, anxieties, and emotions. Meditation has never worked. The concept of being in the present and just watching my thoughts is a feat I have never experienced. I envy those who can achieve this.

However, that day in Seoul, I felt I accomplished a moment of this kind of peace. I stared out the window watching people walking past dressed in their warm coats, some with scarves and others with gloves. The surrounding cafe conversations blended into a hum. It was rewarding to be aware of the calmness I felt. I took a deep breath and vowed to do it again soon.

WHY ALL THE WORRY?

Motherhood creates worry. From the moment you first consider having a baby, it begins. *I'm worried if we don't try now, I'll be too old. I'm worried that I won't be able to fall pregnant.*

Following the miracle, worry over the unborn baby's health arises. *Will he/she be all right? Am I eating all the right foods? Am I putting on too much weight?*

Then after the baby is born, we're off! From the outset, the worry is constant. From baby to adult, the worries change and evolve. I'm at the stage now where I worry if I'm doing everything in my power to support my daughter's career. I still worry about her future.

In reality, there is nothing you can do about this situation. Worry is an unavoidable aspect of parenthood. The key to success lies in being patient and equipped for all possibilities. Prioritise major issues; minor ones can wait. Step back, trust in the work you've done, and let your child take over. Be around, but don't fuss, don't hover, don't probe, don't worry. Things have a way of working out. I've always believed that. We can always find a solution if we talk about it together. The principle I instilled in my daughter as she grew up was, *I prefer not to hear it from others. Whatever happens, good or bad, make sure I'm the first to know. If it's bad, we will work it out.*

If only I could remind myself about these things every day, maybe I could get a good night's sleep instead of staying up worrying.

EXERCISE

An article I read reported that a study of a hundred thousand participants found seven thousand steps a day is enough to combat depression. I had hoped it was for weight loss. This article followed another I read a while ago that suggested six thousand steps, not ten thousand, are sufficient for a healthy lifestyle. Right away, I reduced my Pacer app step target from ten thousand to six. Receiving those inspirational messages to keep going and seeing the confetti fall on the app when I hit the six thousandth step was rewarding. So much more attainable. Today I almost increased the number to seven thousand, but realising it was to prevent depression, I thought I'd do that when I felt that staying in bed was the preferred option to going outside. The people conducting these studies always intrigue me. The only depressing thing I could think of which would directly affect me would result from losing the remnants of my eyebrows, becoming incontinent or incoherent. No number of steps will prevent that. So, I'll stick to the six thousand as my goal and if the confetti doesn't fall today, bad luck.

A few years back, I committed to regular fortnightly payments to a gym to keep myself accountable. Initially, the prospect of attending was exciting. Losing weight and looking fitter was driving me forward. I'd look at myself in the mirror and breathe in. *Cross-fit body builder material I'll never be, but I'll give it a good go.* Attending frequently would be cost effective as well, reducing the cost per class to a minimum if I attended each day. How hard could that be? I'd do it. Sign on the dotted line and move over Jane Fonda.

The first step class I tried was exhausting. I would never have thought that stepping up and down on a small block would be such a killer. The hopping action added to the plight. I attempted the aerobics class next. This was good for me and I went several times. However, I found spin and boxing, among other classes, to be underwhelming.

Swimming was out as I couldn't muster the energy to do the whole shower and change routine, and the spa was the last place I wanted to go. Normally I'd see some large stomached man sitting in there poaching himself while staring at the swimmers. The last thing I needed was to immerse myself in the bubbling pool of other people's germs.

The enthusiasm of my gym membership outweighed the result. After a six-month attempt to bring myself to my peak of fitness, the sessions started becoming more expensive instead of less, because of the number of times I found excuses not to go.

"Are you going to the gym today?" my friend Anna would say when she called in the morning.

"I need to go, I should go, but I don't want to." Would be my regular reply.

"Honestly, just do your walking. You can fit it in whenever."

With that I opted out of the membership, after much to do, as they don't make it easy for people to quit. I vowed never to sign up again. It's just not for me. Jane Fonda, you win.

CAN WE JUST HAVE A NORMAL PICNIC?

"Can I suggest a fun thing we could do this weekend? The weather app is saying it's going to be twenty-five degrees and sunny." A wave of excitement washed over me at the thought of doing something different as I sat with my girlfriends enjoying our weekly coffee meeting.

The girls stopped their conversations and turned to face me. "What about a picnic? We could find a pleasant garden area that offered a walk as well. What do you think?"

Anna was the first to jump at it. "Great, let's all bring something to share. Love the idea."

Isa, Cathy and Elsie were nodding in agreement. Isa already knew what she was going to contribute. "I'll make some mixed sandwiches."

"Is it okay to make some with gluten-free bread?" asked Cathy. She is gluten-free like me.

"Okay. Any preference for types of sandwiches? Good old ham and cheese or chicken and chive?" Isa already sounded perturbed.

"Great," I added. "Is lactose free cheese, okay? No onion for me. Listen, why don't I just make the sandwiches? Might be easier."

Isa pursed her lips and added, "Okay then, I'll get some watermelon and cherries. They're so sweet at the moment."

Elsie, like me, has a fructose issue.

"Those fruits are the worst you can have actually. Any stone fruit as a matter of fact for fructose intolerance. Sorry," I piped in.

"Is it okay to bring berries and pineapple instead? Just that the water-melon and cherries are a bit of an issue for me," Elsie added.

I nodded in agreement, grateful I wasn't the only one bringing this up.

Isa's eyes rolled as she nodded.

Cathy threw in, "I'll make some GF muffins for us."

As it was my suggestion to have this outing, I felt it best I sweeten the deal by adding, "I'll bring the Prosecco and Twisties!"

Anna piped in with, "And I'll bring the coffee."

There was a resounding, “DECAF, please!”

I didn’t dare say lactose free milk.

Cathy closed the conversation by adding, “Can we make sure there’s a toilet nearby, please? I wouldn’t want to be caught in an urgent situation!”

On that one, we were all on the same page.

Germaine Greer was a revolutionary woman, espousing controversial views on femininity and womanhood from the nineteen seventies onwards. Her thinking was unconventional. I am fascinated to hear that her ideas are the basis for many young women's thinking today.

My daughter believes the bees have it down pat. "The females rule and the males only purpose is to mate with the queen bee and then die."

"Sounds like an excellent system. Plus, no boxer shorts to wash or a need to install an industrial fan in the toilet." I was pouring us a glass of Mumm. "Don't men serve a purpose today?" I had to ask.

"No, not really. They've caused all the issues in the world. It's all run by men. White men. If women had been in charge, things would be so different. We have empathy and understanding that men don't."

I couldn't argue the point. I agreed with her.

The dynamics of the male female relationship have changed so much in the past decades. When I see an ad from the fifties – the wife, apron on, full make-up and stilettos, oven mitt in hand –I just laugh to myself. As the husband is welcomed home with a big kiss, he is advised that dinner is ready. Dutifully, the little woman as she would be referred to, would fuss over him. I am grateful for how far we have come. But that was how it was in my marriage decades later and I admit my share of culpability in this. Not as bad as the fifties, but when I married in the early nineties, my attitude reflected my mother's. I made sure dinner was ready for my husband, as we enjoyed an apéritif while the cooking was completed.

A huge point that I couldn't emphasise enough to my daughter was, do not let a man be completely in charge of the bills and finances.

At my age, if a man were to have dinner at home with me, I would expect him to contribute in some form. The ability to pay my own way fills me with gratitude, despite missing the ease of having some dinners covered. As a feminist, as I'd like to believe I am, it is still lovely to have a man make me feel desired and special in both words and gestures. As the Italian saying goes, *Non sei ne carne ne pesce*, (you're neither meat nor fish), meaning neither one nor the other. I am not old-fashioned and neither a man-hater. A happy medium, I'd say.

The belief among young women today, as I've understood from my daughter, is that men are disappointing and that they continue to insist that women take on the role of looking after them. The sentiment is that men know women have the ultimate power as child bearers and have many skills, including multi-tasking, nurturing, empathising, organising and leading. However, when you watch the media, it looks as if men continue to rule over women in government, work environments, religious institutions and at home.

There is the suggestion that if women ruled the world, there would be peace and progress throughout. Of course, this may take several generations to realise, but I would love to be here for that world.

By the second glass of bubbles, the conversation led to a revelation.

"Mum, what about the work they are doing regarding bone marrow? You know they are trying to make sperm from it. If they do, that will really stuff up the system."

That night I had to google it. The work being done in labs experimenting with bone marrow to create female sperm is beyond my understanding. There is much to discover still, but it's being done. The idea of two women having a child, one creating sperm and the other an egg, would raise questions about the role of men. This seems incredible, but society may be inching its way toward female domination. It would make for a great movie script, possibly one I've missed.

I don't find great use for men today. Joy radiates from finding peace within myself. Not having to answer to anyone, compromise or negotiate arguments is a blessing. I find it difficult to come across interesting and challenging men who are smart, witty and sensitive. All others I find boring and hence I'm not interested in pursuing an encounter. At this age, knowing who you are and what you want and desire in everything is freeing. I'm thrilled for those in long-term relationships, but I'm content with my current state. My thought processes might change if I'm lucky enough to live for the next ten or twenty years. It's best never to say never, so I keep myself open to fresh adventures and challenges. Right now, my loved ones are my world, and that feels perfectly right. Happy to be the queen bee in my world.

SWIPING LEFT OR RIGHT?

I am not one for online dating, but I hold no judgement on those that do. I have heard of successful partnerships that have ensued. Unfortunately, the thought of sifting through the copious amount of men who claim to be great catches, brings an enormous sigh.

Years ago, when I divorced, a close girlfriend decided she wanted to put my profile online. I must be transparent and tell you this suggestion was after a fabulous dinner and several drinks. Prosecco in hand,

"Come on, it'll be fun," Paula claimed. "Let's do eHarmony. I'll fill in the profile with you."

I remember looking at her and thinking, *Seriously*?

"Who puts their names on here? I've got no idea who these people are. It's so easy to put in false information." I am not a gambler, and this felt like stepping onto a roulette wheel.

Paula poured me another glass and motioned for me to sit beside her on the rug in front of the coffee table. We looked like two teenagers instead of a couple of middle-aged women about to hurl themselves into the abyss.

"So, the compatibility test asks, 'Why do you think you're single? I have very high expectations of the person I might spend the rest of my life with, or, I wasn't ready before now or I'm too shy to meet people or I just socialise a little.'"

"Please. Spending the rest of my life with a stranger? I'm not even interested enough to spend a day with anyone, let alone a life."

Paula persisted. "The next question says, 'Let's say you and your partner have been invited to a friend's wedding. As you get ready for the party, which thoughts are you most likely to be thinking? Are we going to look good together or have you bought the right gift or I notice I don't enjoy dressing up.'"

"Seriously Paula, answering those options is telling a man I'm either conceited, paranoid or a slob."

She insisted on filling out the copious number of questions. "I'll put my email in, so I'll get the responses and that way I can vet them for you."

In the end, I gave up and let her continue. After at least an hour of these ridiculous scenarios, Paula exclaimed with excitement, "You have twelve matches! Woo-hoo! To see them, you need to pay. Just do the minimum amount and let's take a look."

It was like playing a game. My curiosity got the better of me; I had to see what type of men were there. The good thing was that I was the one to acknowledge the men, and not vice versa. I paid for three months, which was the minimum, and voila, the men appeared.

"Okay.' Paula scrolled down and tried her best to remain excited. "Not sure about this one, or this one."

As I looked at the first profiles, I was a tad dismayed.

"This guy looks so unkempt. Look at this one. Does he need to photograph himself without a shirt?" Peter has three adult children. Bob likes romantic walks along the beach, but he lives in Baccus Marsh.

"You'd have to drive for two hours to see even a glimpse of an ocean." I said. "This is ridiculous."

I allowed Paula to remain optimistic whereas my only glimmer of interest tanked with the comment from Kevin which read, "I want to treat my lady like a queen." Poor Kevin, if I could only write back, *I'm sure you have the best of intentions, but that comment contradicts the other necessities you require from a partner. That she cooks well and loves to garden. Sounds like you need a cook and gardener instead of a partner, Kevin.* They should have a section for Stepford Wives to apply. I'd prefer to poke myself in the eyes with sharp needles rather than spend an evening with most of these men.

I'm not an online dater, I warned you. After three months, Paula had forgotten that the auto renewal wasn't deactivated, so I had to endure another three months of *Ding. Matt has matched with you. Ding, Simon has matched with you, see his profile.* I tried to cancel my subscription, but it wasn't possible until the next three months had run their course. During that time, Paula had come across one match she thought suited me.

"Let's at least go on ONE date. Organise to meet him and we can double date."

Double dating felt less confrontational, so I agreed. I organised for Brett to meet us at the local hotel for a casual dinner. Paula, her husband and I were there on time. Brett appeared wearing a navy suit, open-neck shirt, and a pair of black shoes. He didn't look too bad. Short dark hair and his profile stated he was an accountant.

He was polite, chatty, and seemed interested in me. I thought perhaps I was too harsh in my judgement about online dating. When the waiter brought over the wine list, Brett took it and asked Paula's husband if he had any preference. Once I piped up saying a red would go well, he began pontificating about the selection on offer. At last, he settled on an expensive option, and when it was presented, he did the full sommelier impersonation. Sniff, swirl, and mouthwash. Thank goodness he swallowed and didn't spiff it back into his glass.

The dinner was quite nice considering it was getting to know a complete stranger. The conversation was bland. He lacked a sense of humour, which was one of my fundamental requirements.

The clincher came at the end of the meal. When the bill arrived, he took out his phone and calculated the cost of his meal. There was no suggestion of contributing to the cost of my meal, even though I was prepared to pay for my own.

But what was worse, he offered nothing for the wine. He put down his money for his meal, and I looked at Paula. We divided the rest and after dividing by three, I ended up paying more than he did.

I couldn't wait for the subscription to expire.

BAD LUCK, OR IN DUTCH, PECH

My dearest friend had booked a mother-daughter cruise from Amsterdam to Budapest two years ago. Unfortunately, because of her daughter's study commitments, she couldn't go, and they brought it forward to last year. I had been wanting something exciting to do and after a chat over lunch, my friend made a phone call to the travel agent and my daughter and I were booked in.

"I secured you the last cabin," the agent announced.

"I'm thrilled beyond words." My friend's beaming smile made it clear she was overjoyed that we were joining them.

"August seems a long way away. It's only January. I'm sure it will go quickly and we'll be off." I matched her enthusiasm, and the four of us knew this would be one for the memory bank.

Despite attempting to pack lightly, my daughter and I each had a full suitcase on the day of our departure. I didn't enjoy the flight over much. I only slept for an hour the entire flight because the airline's economy seats were tiny. In case of an evacuation, they'd have to hand out can openers first. Arriving in Amsterdam in the morning, the plan was to stay awake as long as possible to acclimatise to the new time zone. We walked around for three hours, taking in the magic and beauty of this city. I had booked to stay an extra day so that we could make the most of the experience and therefore arrived earlier than my friend. As we dragged our weary feet back to the hotel, I spotted a supermarket close by. Once we dropped off the new knitwear we had bought, I lay on the bed and began feeling that sleep was imminent.

"Are you hungry?" I asked my girl. "I'll go down and get a few things from the supermarket to nibble on?"

"That's a great idea, Mum. Can you get some snacky stuff?"

"Sure." I got organised. As I left our room, I spotted the stairwell on the left and thought it was a good idea considering I'd been sitting for the last day. I headed down. Once I reached the ground floor, the double doors to the foyer were closed. Opening one door, I was expecting to step into the same level foyer, and was not at all prepared for the ten-inch step up which appeared. Butting my foot against it, I lost my balance and sidestepped to the ground like a drunken hobo, straight onto a metal coffee machine which had been left sitting against the wall. I hit my left side hard enough to make me look for blood.

Staggering back onto my feet, I took the lift back up to the room, all the while trying to catch my breath.

"I've just fallen and I think I've really hurt myself." My expression said it all.

My daughter shot up out of bed.

"We need to go to a hospital. Best I check what I've done."

The hotel front desk was very helpful. The difference in Amsterdam is that you need to book an emergency doctor, unlike in Australia where you just join the queue at a hospital emergency department.

The prognosis was three broken ribs. No wonder it was so painful. I was given very strong painkillers. Five hours after my arrival in Amsterdam, I was already experiencing the hospital system.

The next morning when my friend arrived, her daughter raced over to hug me and I threw my arms forward in a motion to stop her.

"How was yesterday? Did you both have a ball?" my friend asked.

"You'll never guess where we went last night."

WITH AGE COMES COMPLAINTS

As you age, you seem to find more and more to be unhappy about. The complaints become part of the daily ritual.

I have a good breadth of experience to refer to, as the women in my immediate family range from ages twenty-eight to ninety-one. Guess which one complains most? Yep, the ninety-one-year-old. And the twenty-eight-year-old tells ME off for complaining too much.

"Why did you do that?" my twenty-eight-year-old said to me yesterday morning when I walked in grimacing and puffing with two heavy shopping bags.

"Boy, these are so heavy. We were missing something to drink, so I bought some bottles. Two bottles of tonic water, a coconut water, a bottle of cordial and then I saw that the four pack of zero spritz were on sale, so I bought two."

"You didn't have to buy them all at once."

"I know. Just thought I'd buy them in one hit."

"Then don't complain."

Bang. There you are. Don't complain. In other words, you chose to be so ridiculous as to carry all that in one go, it's on you.

That's true. It's quite easy to slip in annoyances, grievances and dissatisfaction. I think I have been tainted by my mother as conversations with her mainly revolve around complaints and negativity now. I don't recall her complaints being as prevalent as they are now after Dad's passing. I'm guessing he may have taken the brunt of them.

"Good morning. Isn't it cold today? I wasn't expecting this weather." Or, "Did you see the news last night? The violence that's happening here is terrible." Or, "The fellow that does the garden is hopeless. I have to show him every weed to pull out, otherwise he doesn't see it." Or "I can't stand that everything happens to me." Or, "Where is that brand I used to buy? I can't believe they're not making it anymore."

Just a few of the comments that greet me each day.

I don't recall having too many things to complain about in my twenties, but undoubtedly, they'll increase with age.

SKIMMING

I feel like a stone skimming on the surface of life. I don't delve deep on life's issues and at the same time I'm not shallow. When I was diagnosed with cancer I never once asked, why me? In fact, my question was, what do I need to do to prevent this happening again? I didn't overthink what I needed to face but rather took the attitude of "bring it on". Is there a better way to handle it when you are fighting for your life?

Many concerning events are occurring in the world right now. I keep up to date with everything but allow myself time to switch off. My off switch has been working overtime of late. I wouldn't describe it as apathy, just survival. After going through the fear and panic of Covid, especially being locked up for close to a year in Melbourne, I've decided that caution should take the place of fear.

I like the idea of skimming. It feels light, joyful and fun. I'm going to keep trying to remain on the surface of life for as long as I can.

LOOKING FORWARD TO BEING RUDE

You often hear, *Don't worry, they're old. Let it go.*

I can't wait to take full advantage of being incredibly rude, entitled, selfish, and completely obnoxious as I get older. There's also the benefit of pretending to be helpless. To make people move out of my way, I'll need a walker, or even a motorised walker, depending on how annoying I'd like to be. Then it'll be standing in a queue with a sad face waiting for someone to signal for me to move ahead of them to pay. Fantastic!

My mother finally decided to sell her home at the end of last year and the transition needed to begin. The family home was a treasured place for us all and my mother struggled with the decision, but realistically, it had become too much to look after. It was a large three-storey home which my father had designed sixty years ago.

As a lead-up to the sale, I suggested that my mother begin purging anything she felt was not needed anymore.

"You need to go through cupboard by cupboard and see if there are things you no longer need. That way, we can transport only the items you want to keep."

"Most of my things are good."

"Yes, they are good Mum. However, there is no way you'll be able to fit a three-storey home into a two-bedroom apartment."

With that being said, I felt assured Mum would slowly and methodically remove all items not required at the new residence.

I couldn't have been more wrong. As

we got closer to the removalist van's arrival, the family started transporting items to the new place. Surely, having only the basics to move, it would be a speedy affair? On the day of the removalists, I couldn't be there. Sick at home, I knew the rest of the family would make sure it would go smoothly.

TEN hours later, the van finally left. I couldn't believe it. A two and half meter buffet unit my mother insisted on taking with her, ended up having to be hoisted over the balcony as it couldn't go up the stairwell or the elevator.

The next few days were a disaster. Each day we would go to the old home, I'd open a cupboard and it would be filled with her things.

"Mum, I can't believe how much STUFF you have, and that it wasn't packed. Can you go through this one now?" I implored her as we opened a bedroom cupboard. At the bottom of the wardrobe were trays of costume jewellery.

"Take it all and I'll go through it at home and throw anything out from there," Mum instructed me.

This was her mantra for all the cupboards. I bagged all the jewellery and carrying it nearly dislocated my shoulder as I hoisted it to the front door.

"Can you feel the weight of this, please?"

"Oh my goodness, it's so heavy."

"This is the jewellery of a ninety-one-year old frail little old lady, who can hardly walk!" My sarcastic tone made my mother break out in laughter.

"Stop, don't make me laugh. I have to go to the toilet."

"Ten kilos of jewellery. If you decide to wear these, the weight of a couple of those necklaces will topple you forward."

And with that, we both laughed whole-heartedly, so much so that Mum didn't quite make it in time to the toilet. That's another story.

As the days passed, the piles of things she wanted to take across to the apartment grew. Every-time she looked at something, it was the same response.

"I might need it. Let me see at the apartment first and then I'll decide."

The piles grew and grew and each time she looked at them, she said, "I feel like vomiting."

"You wanted to take it all," I'd reply. "You can be on the next episode of hoarders."

She laughed. “I know. I never removed things, only added to them. In this house, everything had its place.”

And it did. The house was always in order, clean and meticulously organised.

Perhaps that’s why I purge so often? Could it be a psychological response to having too much of everything?

I’m still going to pursue minimalism. One day.

I felt reinvigorated to expand my coffee options at home. Toward the back of my cupboard, the Nespresso machine lay sideways as if it had had a rough night or been the victim of a hit and run. It looked pathetic considering it had taken prime position when I bought it a few years ago. During COVID, I laid it to rest as stepping out to buy capsules became difficult and I would not order everything online. I converted to the Smeg filter coffee machine.

Back to my poor abandoned Nespresso. My daughter expressed a desire to have a different option, so I placed it proudly back in its original position. Having decided it was best to descale before re-using it, I found it had stopped working. Long story short, I had to purchase a new machine.

The point being, I now have a new Nespresso machine, a large Smeg drip filter machine, another smaller glass paper drip filter, a small pink Italian coffee percolator, a filter coffee plunger, an obscene number of coffee sachet alternatives bought from Korea and what do I make for myself in the morning? A decaf instant Moccona coffee.

THE STORAGE CAGE

The storage cages in my garage are a disgrace. Every so often, I wander down with a bag of items I feel sorry for and shove them in alongside the other losers. Most of the things in the cages had purpose upstairs once upon a time. Now they have become part of the disgraced bunch, not quite ready for immediate elimination, but that destiny awaits. Items sitting on death row. The day will come when they will be called.

A few pieces, like the suitcases, know they have been spared. They come in and out often, so they sit safe in the knowledge they still serve a purpose.

If they could speak, the conversation would go something like this,

I'm not sure how long we'll be around, cause there used to be a purple suitcase, but now it's gone. None of us are safe!

It's hopeless. We've been rolling around for some time now. I used to be taut and shiny. Look at me now, stretched, scuffed and hideous. There's a check-in sticker still on my side from 5 years ago. If I make it

through the night, promise, I'm going to walk!

You mean roll.

About twelve months ago, I had a good sort through and had the cages looking lean and accessible. Today they are piled high with lumps and bumps, old bedsheets thrown over the piles to hide my shame. The mantra of, "I might sell this at a trash and treasure market" HAS to stop. I need to remind myself that waking at 4 am and trudging to the market in darkness, hauling boxes out of the car and laying them on a wobbly trestle table beside the hanging rail full of my clothes that are now being handed on for five or ten dollars apiece, is not as much fun as it used to be for the meagre profit one makes at these markets. Risking Melbourne's unpredictable weather is also a turn off. In years gone by, I've been scorched, blown and torrentially rained on.

I vow to head to those cages soon. I can hear the cries already.

REFUSE

It's a nicer word, refuse. Much nicer than garbage or rubbish. But rubbish is what we accumulate constantly and consistently. Just think for a moment about the things that you've had in your life that have eventually become rubbish. You just need to look at old photos and remember the outfit you wore, or the furniture in the background. Clothes, shoes, bags, jewellery, furniture, kitchenware, bed linen and so much more. These were all so important at first, then took second priority as new items came into the house. Their imprisonment in garage cages concluded with their eventual removal from the house.

I tried to recoup some of my losses by selling items on Gumtree and eBay. Passing my rubbish on to other people, who eventually on-sold it to others. The circle of rubbish. I justify my actions by thinking that passing on my rubbish prolongs its life, which is better for sustainability. In the short term, yes, but it will all end up being refuse. It's inevitable.

Nothing lasts forever, not even us.

BYGONE ERA OF BEING NURTURING

The nurturer has been slapped out of me over the years. I used to enjoy looking after my husband, preparing tasty meals, keeping the house looking great. Twenty years ago, the fuss and bother I went through to prepare dinner parties and family functions, took hours. I had colour themes, table decorations, presentation platters, and candles twinkling alongside the sparkling glassware. I belonged in an episode of the *Dick Van Dyke Show* or *Here's Lucy* (two of my favourite shows ever). I'd laugh seeing the women of those days dressed beautifully every day, make-up, hair all perfect. Some even wore high heels around the house. In my case, not only would I be in crippling pain, but they would pose a definite tripping hazard. The woman's focus was their husbands. The old "pipe and slippers at the door". This seems far from the expectations of today.

While I'm still houseproud and care about presentation, I'm not interested in preparing dinners, washing and dealing with a man's needs. The nurturing side of me has evaporated. If there were a man around today, it would be take me as I am, one eyebrow, stomach roll, and downward facing boobs. For that reason, I see no need to bring a man into the house. Unless, of course, he resembles Clooney, is Clooney's age and has Clooney's money. I might put on the heels for that one.

Teatless udders really, we call them bye byes as you only notice them when you wave bye bye, Dame Edna.

Look at your fadoobadahs, Kim. Wasn't that a classic Kath and Kim moment, the sound of Kath's disgust at her daughter's upper arm skin overhang? I don't think I'd ever heard of that term until that marvellous show. The fadoobs were a generational part of the body that were laughed at, mocked and toyed within our family as well. It all started with my maternal grandmother. I loved her very much, and on the occasion when I was lucky enough to visit her in Trieste, Italy, the fadoobs were a laughing point. As a little girl, I was fascinated by the pendulous skin on my Nonna's upper arms. When we'd sit together, I'd flick her arms, and she'd loving say, *basta, basta,* (enough, enough) as she shrugged her shoulders, pulling her arm away. We'd both laugh. A lovely memory for me.

The next victim was Mum. As her fadoobs became apparent, I repeated the same procedure with her. We would reminisce about her mother and so the ritual continued.

The time has come for my turn. The other day, my daughter did exactly the same thing to me. She wasn't privy to my previous fadoob invasions, yet she felt compelled to give mine a good swing. It's in the family genes. That there was significant pendulum movement brought a smile to my face. This is what it felt like for Nonna and Mum. Things have a way of making a full circle. Basta! Basta!

Think of a kilo of sausage meat being stuffed into its casing. That was me last week trying to find an appropriate garment to enhance my posterior. David Jones department store has an extensive collection and is my go-to for underwear, so I headed off to buy a pair of flattering underwear for future use.

"I'd like to find something to help give my backside a tighter look, please."

I was too embarrassed to say, "Could you give me anything that will hoist up my arse and make it look two sizes smaller?"

"Absolutely." I admired the sales-girl's enthusiasm and confidence. I don't think she knew who she was dealing with.

"I don't like anything too tight, cause I'd like to still breathe as normally as possible."

"Is it for a special occasion?" the slim, twenty-something enquired.

"Not really. I'm just organising a back-up, in case I do have somewhere to go one day." Now I really sounded pathetic.

After careful consideration, the lovely salesgirl handed me three pairs of full briefs, two nude and one black. I'm sure she was thinking, give her a black one as its slimming and might give a better illusion.

One nude pair looked only big enough for a toddler over nappy pants. Surely the salesgirl couldn't be serious. I looked at the size and yes, size 12 as I'd requested. With diminished confidence, I entered one of the busy change rooms. I made sure to secure the door, as an unexpected accidental door opening would be scarring for any stranger. I was able to put one leg through, but the next was impossible. I struggled to wiggle the toddler pants halfway up my thighs and the circulation in my legs slowed significantly. I thought it best to whip them off before my legs turned blue.

The next nude pair looked more generous. Taking the pair in hand, I wriggled them up to encompass my bum but the leg circumference cut into my thighs, giving the impression I was pouring out from either side, looking like an inflated buoy. The waist band was so tight that the muffin top it created looked like the oozing of cheese after the toastie has been left on the grill too long.

One more pair to go, the girl turned up and asked, "How are you going?"

"All good" was my response instead of, *hopeless so far. I don't think I'm cut out for this bum girdle situation.*

All hope was left to the last pair of black briefs. Nothing brief about them, mind you. They would give Bridget Jones a run for her money. They looked huge, yet tight. The legs fitted well, but the waistline repeated the same ooze, resembling sausage meat in casing. I pulled the band out, tucking in the bits, but I was sure if these were worn under a dress, there was no way to hide the appearance of my body being separated into two sections. Very sad.

I thanked the girl for her help and walked away knowing that the solution lay in me accepting that the bits were now out and it was fruitless trying to put them back in. Give them freedom to roam. I refuse to sit at a function, feigning interest as I begin to black out from reduced blood flow, which will undoubtedly create digestive problems and a possible yeast infection. Let it all hang out.

WHERE WILL I BE?

Projecting forward feels exciting. Having reached this age is wonderful. As years go by, I don't focus on the numbers so much as how I feel. Even though the body is showing wear and tear, there is an optimistic side of me that wants to be excited about what lies ahead. The seventies, eighties and possibly the nineties? Who knows? Coming to accept the changes in my body and my lifestyle have been cathartic, and while more changes lie ahead, I will front these with acceptance and gratitude. "Bring it on" has become my mantra after all these years. As I've navigated through cancer, marriage, divorce, motherhood, ailing parents and the death of my father, these life events have shaped me to be who I am.

Now is the time to embrace the strong, positive future which I hope lies ahead. The burning questions I have are few.

Will I wear bright red lipstick again?

Will my scepticism for Botox change?

Will I date a forty-something?

Will I channel Iris Apfel and wear

multiple layered chunky jewellery, enormous glasses and out-there clothes?

It's all in the stars and I'm up for anything. As long as a visit to the doctor doesn't end in *I've found a lump.* That's when my new mantra will kick in, BRING IT ON!

THE GOOD 'OL BOD

I saw a photo of myself in my twenties the other day when I headed to that infamous cage to begin the decluttering process. The first box I came across was full of photo albums. I recall the meticulous way I'd take my reels to the Kodak kiosk and anxiously await the yellow sleeve which held my travel memories. It was exciting to review which shots were going to make it into the prized album. With a box of albums in hand, I took myself back upstairs, made a coffee and sat on the couch, ready for a look back in time.

In photo one, I was in a bikini at a beach resort. The bikini was burnt orange, my hair was significantly fuller and wavy, and my tan a golden brown. The lush red, orange, and green plants made me think the photo was taken in Thailand. It made me feel like I was looking at a different person. I was struck by how rapidly my body has changed. I was thankful for this photo, as it reminded me of Moira's advice to Stevie in Schitts Creek: *Take a thousand naked pictures of yourself now. You may currently think, oh, I'm too spooky, or nobody wants to see these tiny boobies. But believe me, one day you will look at those photos with much kinder eyes and say, dear God, I was a beautiful thing.*

Young, perky, flat stomach and tanned. Today I recognise my boobs left after I had my daughter without even saying goodbye. Now they've gone the full National Geographic.

But in recognition of my body and its evolution, I'd like it to take a bow. Well done on keeping up with me through thick and thin. Thanks for providing a nurturing environment for my daughter at the beginning of her life. A huge acknowledgment for the courage it took to fight off cancer. Round of applause from the audience for healing well after my broken knee. Congratulations on your unrelenting dedication and determination in keeping me alive.

I appreciate you and your support.

Take another bow.

THE ICE CREAM TRUCK

Hearing the faint sound of Mr Whippy rounding the corner at the end of my street made me stop in my tracks as a five-year-old. I'd yell to Mum, "Mr Whippy! Mr Whippy!" and make my five-year-old legs sprint as quickly as they could to the front gate. The fear that he would chime straight past my house was unbearable. Standing on tiptoe at the driveway gate, stretching myself as far as I could to spot the musical truck approaching, brought the taste buds alive. Mr Whippy had a good customer base in my street, as there were eight children in the immediate vicinity.

Thruppence in hand, I waited for the smallest vanilla soft-serve to arrive. It didn't matter that the soft-serve would often be too soft and dribble down my forearm as I tried to ingest it before the whole thing collapsed. Nope, it didn't matter at all. It was the best ice-cream ever.

That chiming sound today still brings back the fondest of memories.

CLIP CLOP

Having lived through the technology era for quite some time now, it's strange to think that as a child, I experienced the clip-clopping of a horse-drawn milk delivery truck. I often awoke to the sound of an approaching horse before dawn. From my floor length bedroom windows overlooking the street, I would hear, *Whoa* and watch the horse obey and come to a stop. I jumped across from one window to the other, for a good view of the horse. He would adjust his hooves and his head, the mane glistening in the moonlight on a clear night. The clinking of the bottles would break the silence, as two full bottles of milk replaced the empties in the metal bottle carrier. I'd watch as the milkman delivered to our neighbours across the road, then jumped into the front of the open-sided truck, with a, *Tsk, Tsk*, and they would clip clop down the hill until the next stop.

THE WONDERFUL WORLD OF PARENTING

A persistent cough had been nagging me, so I thought it best to have it checked at my local clinic. I was sitting in the open reception area, waiting for my name to be called, immersed in an article on Ozempic and its possible side effects. I gave myself an internal high five for not contemplating using it.

I didn't notice a father and his children had presented themselves at the payment area. He had come out from seeing a doctor and the children were unscathed, which was a pleasant relief, as so many find the entire experience terrifying and often end wailing. The father was in his early thirties or thereabouts, his daughter around four and the brother, two and a half.

"Dillon, stay still. Charlotte, don't run around." Dad was attempting to answer the receptionist's questions.

"Which doctor did you see?"

"Charlotte, come here. Dillon, don't you run off."

At that point, Dillon ran full speed

toward the exit, which leads out to the street. Dillon was laughing wholeheartedly and Charlotte joined him. Dad called out both names as the children shrilled in delight at the chase. Dad swooped up Dillon in his arms and returned with Charlotte to the reception desk.

"Sorry, which doctor was this for?"

"Rahami," Dad called out the doctor's name as Dillon and Charlotte took off again, Dad in pursuit, laughing as well this time.

"Both of you need to wait with me. Daddy needs to pay."

Pay? That's nothing to do with us, they were thinking. Our job is to give you hell.

As Dad removed his wallet, the children played around his legs. Charlotte instigated the twenty-yard dash this time. Dillon stood watching, then thought he may as well make a run for it because Dad was only calling Charlotte's name.

Dad had to run full speed again, this time taking one child in each arm. The novelty has worn off and he stated, "You are both going to be in trouble when we get home."

Back at reception, Dad finally paid

and as he was waiting for the Medicare refund to go through, Dillon took off again. Charlotte stayed this time. As Dad called for him to stop, Charlotte jumped up and down as if she'd just seen an ice-cream truck.

Dad came back holding Dillon, saying, "You are both going straight to bed when we get home." Mind you it was around four thirty at this point.

"Dad no! Dillon started it." Straight under the bus goes Dillon.

"You've both been naughty. Straight to bed."

The mood changed and the children stood crestfallen beside Dad as he completed the transaction. Then the choir began. Both children cried, howled, and began screaming, "I don't want to go to bed," in tandem chorus.

Unbelievable noise continued even after Dad left. For five more minutes, the children's cries were heard as their father stood outside the door, scolding them for their naughtiness. As they left onto the shopping strip, the escalation wound down. With a do you believe it look, the waiting patients glanced at each other.

I timed this parent's exit from the clinic. It took him eight minutes.

My childhood came to mind as I sat there. I would never have dreamed of moving even a few feet away from Mum's side if she were paying for something. If I were told to stand still, I'd stand still. When I was told to say hello, I'd say hello. I would never ask for anything if we were visiting someone. I was taught that I could quietly ask Mum if I needed something, then wait to be offered something. Then I'd need to look at Mum for her approval, and politely accept. At a restaurant, I needed to sit where I was told, eat what was put in front of me, and never disturb the other patrons.

What has changed so much today that I sound like I was raised in a military reform school instead of a loving household? What happened to parenting over the years that has produced children such as those I witnessed at the doctor's clinic? It doesn't look like fun anymore. In my teaching days, I saw children yell at their parents, scream at them and refuse to do as they were asked. How grateful I am to have passed that stage in my life so I'm not confronted with children who need constant positive reinforcement and resilience boosting.

ARE WE CREATING LITTLE MONSTERS?

Children today are being rewarded for everything. It used to be a challenge to win a race at school on sports day. The prize for working hard and achieving your best was a ribbon. The blue, red or green ribbon. I remember giving it my all just so I could later walk around with a ribbon flapping as I sashayed past my friends. I won a few ribbons during my schooling as I enjoyed sports.

Today every child receives a ribbon. First, second, third, fourth, fifth and participant. The participant ribbon is a dark pink colour and most of the girls want that one, forget the others. Prizes and accolades are constantly given to the students. They are told that they have done well. Classroom reports must be written in a positive tone, with parent-teacher interviews conducted in a positive light. In my day, the teacher was to the point, stating where the student needed improvement and where they were lacking. I received a few *talks too much in class* and *needs to focus more*, on my report cards.

I believe showing children that striving for success is a good thing. Can we bring back the first, second and third ribbons only? And reduce the constant reassurance and praise for every small thing a child does.

When my daughter was young, I praised her all the time. Positive reinforcement. This was the era when children were given a voice; they were included in decision making and offered a plethora of explanations, reasoning and understanding. This was the latest theory for raising a child. It was a different time from the *children must be seen and not heard* I grew up in.

We had evolved into building confidence, character, and ability in our children or so we thought. I think my daughter has turned out well, even with a few dark pink ribbons thrown in. Having said that, I return to the fact that less praise is needed today. Keep children striving and reaching for goals and make them work for rewards. Allow them to find their passions. Whether they excel in sport, music, art or academics, a *slow and easy wins the race* is a good lesson to impart. In a society where information is acquired in an instant, teaching our children that taking time to achieve greatness in anything they choose to pursue, will provide a great sense of achievement.

Sorry, you will not get a ribbon for every race. There are a lot of races you will not win in life, so get ready.

Honesty is the Best Policy

Honesty is the best policy.

Is it?

Really?

Who was the person who invented this saying and why did they?

How many of us are blatantly honest all the time? I wish!

How often do you hear people say, "Well, can I be honest?" I always feel like saying, "No. Lie to me, please." It's rare that I can speak freely and honestly, with friends especially. I'm always conscious of hurting people's feelings, offending them (which I can do), or disappointing them. Comedians speak the truth, and their honesty makes us laugh because we are too scared to say it out loud, even though we might think it. They do it for us.

In the old days of comedy, the Lucille Ball era, simple hilarious skits and physical comedy situations reflected life at that time. It was brilliant and I still enjoy rewatching these shows over and over. Today Ricky Gervais' humour offends everyone and I love it. The more offensive the better for him, yet it's always done in an intelligent way.

I'm too scared to be as offensive, so I'll stick to what I know. Being sixty-six is terrific even though some bits are starting to fall off, patience is waning, people are more annoying, family is taxing and sex is but a memory. When it all boils down to it, not relying on any man "to complete me" and not wanting to be completed is empowering. Time to be honest here.

I'm sixty-six and loving it, Jerry!

⇢ THE CLIMB ⇠

I picture my life as a visual sequence of a towering mountain alternating with a massive stepladder. At the start of the climb, I felt enthusiastic, emboldened and excited, and raced up the mountain. The rush to the top left behind piles of rocks and pebbles. As the years passed, I climbed with added caution, wary of existing pitfalls but nevertheless exhilarated. Marriage makes me lose my footing, but by desperately holding onto the sides of the ladder, I place my feet on a solid rung and keep climbing. My daughter's birth gave a fresh spring to my step; however, the distance between the rungs seemed to be getting larger. Right after that, a huge, cancerous boulder came hurtling down the mountain, straight for me. Fortunately, I threw myself to the side and only sustained internal injury. I evaded death. After what seemed a long pause, I regained my strength to continue my trek to the top.

From that vantage point, I could see far. I knew the climb down was going to be challenging, but I was ready for it. The aches and pains of various ailments were surfacing, but this would not deter a safe journey. As I continue to venture down the mountain, I do not know where the pitfalls will lie, where I will stumble, or when I will need help. It's an unknown journey and a safe landing is not promised. At sixty-six, I have only stumbled on a few loose rocks, and remain standing despite uneasy footing.

As I progress along the long path home, I listen to the sound of the birds, feel the warmth of the sun and appreciate the challenges and joys of my journey to the peak. My dream is to remain on solid footing for a long time. However, I will accept and deal with any boulders that come my way. Let's go.

This is a recurrence in my day to day life. It didn't just start recently; it's a brain fog that has progressively gotten worse. I read that chemotherapy adds to brain fog, as does pregnancy, and then there are the hormonal changes that fog things up as well. Given these factors, I should be in a complete pea-soup by now. Adding to the fact that my memory hasn't been brilliant since I was younger, you could say that lucidity has not been my forte. When I'm trying to explain a thought, or recall a name or place or person, I stumble, become lost for words and at times, somewhat incoherent. If I'm in company other than family and close friends, I hear myself and think, *Woman, get a grip. What are you trying to say? You sound like an imbecile.* Yesterday I had to diarise the fact that the food delivery box was arriving that morning.

"What do you want for dinner tonight?" I asked my daughter. I had already started huffing and puffing, thinking I needed to plan and organise another evening meal.

"Don't you remember that the delivery is coming today?"

"Oh yes. I forgot." My mistake, admitting my forgetfulness.

"But you wrote it on your phone yesterday."

"I know." What else can you come back with? *Your mum's brain has become a sieve? With me, the nuclear codes are in excellent hands. Never have cause to use them though, as I'd have no recollection of what they are or where they are or how to use them.*

It's such a frustrating ailment. As a single parent, I still need to have my daughter respect me. Honestly, how can she when her mother struggles to remember the hotel we stayed in Korea only two months earlier? Not two years, two months. I'm forever scrolling old emails with keywords to prompt a sigh of relief. Found it. I have discovered that men do not understand brain fog. In a past relationship, my partner would preface many sentences with, *You won't remember this,* or, *You don't remember them, do you?* Even if I did remember, I'd still be given the eye roll and be told, *Yeah, okay, you remember.*

I recall details sometimes, but now

I've become a lost cause, all confidence vanquished. I may as well be driving through dense snow with a blindfold. When I googled forgetfulness and its link to dementia, I took solace because I wasn't forgetting why I left the house this morning or having difficulty following a recipe or making a cup of tea. It's just brain fog. I have fuzzy-headedness and poor concentration. Focus, woman, focus! Let there be light.

⇉ AN IDEAL PARTNERSHIP ⇇

As you age, you become set in your ways, a statement that has been used over and over, for good reason. With aging, your threshold for compromise becomes narrower and narrower. Many things become evident when considering a live-in arrangement at this age. I have many requirements. Some houses already offer dual vanity units in the bathroom. However, do I want to watch and listen to someone gargle, spit, and expel guttural phlegm? Homes boast separate walk-in closets and two toilets in different parts of the house, dedicating one to the partner who needs absolute privacy and full proofing from the rest of the house. There have been situations where an industrial fan the size of the East Link Tunnel wouldn't have been large enough to eradicate the smell. Then there are the arguments around the temperature controls in the car and in the house. *I'm too hot, I'm too cold. Can you reduce the gale force wind? We are not in a sauna.* My preference is for the temperature to be around twenty-three degrees and for the fan to be running at a low speed. A gentle, fresh breeze. I've had requests for hurricane speed winds of sub-freezing temperatures during summer. Some beds offer separate controls for curvature change. An inclined sleeping position for your partner may lead to an accidental nose-breaking experience if you turn in your sleep.

Having to compromise on so many issues tells me that living with a partner is very challenging at this age. In my dream home of the past, the master suite would have boasted two bedrooms, each with its own walk-in closet and bathroom. For most nights, there'd be a nearby second bedroom to ensure a good night's sleep. Today, my dream home comprises a bathroom, bedroom, climate control, and a temporary door key which expires at midnight. All visitors will vacate the premises at that time. A girl needs her beauty sleep.

ONCE A MOTHER ALWAYS A MOTHER

Taking my mother for coffee yesterday morning reminded me that a mother is always a mother, no matter what age the children are, even at sixty-six.

Stepping outside to begin our walk to the cafe, Mum said, "It's cold today. You must be cold. You didn't wear enough; would you like a cardigan?"

"Thanks, but no. I'm fine. I'm always too hot, plus it's humid today."

"You don't want to catch a cold with this chill."

"You need to catch the germs, not the fresh breeze to get a cold."

"I know, but still, you never know."

And so, we could go on, but I can never win the argument. It is like the pyjamas I received for Christmas in size large.

"I hope you like them. I loved the colour, and they were in your size."

"Thanks Mum. Perhaps next time you could buy medium because I haven't been large in many years."

"But you always wore large."

"Yes, I did years ago. Now I'm medium. Soon I'll start shrinking and be a small." I tried to lighten the conversation before she started saying I must be mistaken.

At a dinner I ordered a gin and tonic. Mum was astounded.

"I didn't know you drank gin," said in such a way that I felt that I was a recovering alcoholic who had just ordered a full bottle of gin to take to the local park bench.

"Yes, now and then, I enjoy something different."

"It's very strong. It doesn't affect you?" again, said in a way that made me feel implicated as a wayward woman who downed shot after shot until I was legless.

"No Mum, it's fine." I wouldn't dare share with her that I've been known to have two G n T's followed by a glass of wine with dinner. I'm sure she would find some obscure relative in our family who died of alcohol poisoning to compare me to. Shhhh!

WOMANHOOD

Women are to be admired, respected and applauded. They deserve accolades for what they achieve. Women go through their lives being everything to everyone and so often their achievements go unnoticed or unrecognised. They forge through marriages, divorces, partnerships, children and workplaces. Then they are faced with health issues, menopause and aging parents. The strength it takes to undertake all these duties and bodily changes is huge. I'm proud to be a woman and at this age and stage of my life I have handled all of the above mentioned. Let's give ourselves a standing ovation. We certainly deserve it.

FOOD

Why is it I have become so bored with food? The plausible answer is that I repeatedly turn to the same things. How often have I mentioned the can of tuna tossed onto a salad? I find cooking tedious, having to put so much time and effort into choosing meals, preparing and cleaning up. I see food as an essential element of life, not a joy and neither a pleasure. Get it in and get it out. Sorry, but that's the reality.

Mind you, I appreciate the time and effort people go to when they prepare wonderful meals. How is it that some people grow up with a passion for putting flavours together and others, like myself, could stick to the same flavour over and over. The beauty, intricacy and flavour chefs achieve in their cooking astounds me. The study involved in becoming a Cordon Bleu or Michelin chef status is considerable. I'd poke my eyes out with scissors rather than attend those classes.

I could employ a personal chef. That would be ideal as I know I could instruct them to prepare tasty yet healthy meals.

That is a dream, along with a house cleaner, of course.

Of late, I have resorted to having a sandwich for dinner alongside a salad. Sandwiches have always been my go-to for lunch and I thought, who said you can't eat a sandwich for dinner? Now I look forward to a toastie or tuna on toast or scrambled egg on toast for dinner. I am blending the whole eating day into a series of continual breakfasts and lunches. Dinner has slipped out of the trio and becomes only relevant a few times a week.

Sandwiches all day, every day? Pure bliss.

SLUMBER

The last time I remember having a "full night's" sleep would be around thirty to forty years ago. And by full night, I mean at least a seven-to-eight-hour full-length feature. My sleep pattern today you could classify as vignettes. I'm asleep, I'm awake. Awake, awake, awake, awake, asleep. Awake, drag the body around the house or outdoors, lunch and most probably asleep again. Startles awake and proceeds through to the evening portion of the day where the thought of bed is enticing. Repeat.

In my twenties, sleep was sound and extended. I recall Mum complaining that I would sleep until midday in my late teens and early twenties. Therefore, I have proof that it did happen. At age thirty-two, I married and the sleep decline began. I was married to a chainsaw. Every night the snoring began, mouth open, nose flaring. It is difficult to get used to and I think that at some point you become so sleep deprived that they could have been drilling for oil under the bed and I wouldn't have heard it. There had to be at least a couple of hours of quality sleep squeezed in some nights. I recall lying beside my sleeping husband giving a gentle nudge, then a firmer shove while whispering the soft words 'turn over,' while I really wanted to slap him across the head and double leg him straight off the bed.

Pregnancy brings the next stage of discomfort while trying to rest. I had to train myself from being a stomach sleeper to a side sleeper, all the while conjuring up pictures of inserting tampons in my husband's nostrils or not forcibly placing a pillow over his face. Just to cut out the noise, let's not read into this.

Once the baby arrived, I'm sure my husband's sleep became deeper but mine was so light I would wake if a fly walked past on the opposite wall. It's incredible how a woman's sleep pattern changes. I distinctly recall scooping up my baby girl in my arms and taking her downstairs, so allowing my husband the luxury of a full night's rest. Instead, I did a mini marathon each night around three-thirty to four am, up and down the living room. As soon as the baby finally fell asleep, I would tiptoe into her room, placing her down in a slow-motion bend toward her mattress and gently removing one arm at a time. I would make it to her door or just outside, when the cry often began again. Repeat procedure with the bonus of collapsing on the couch downstairs after another walk, fearing that I would fall into a deep sleep and my arms would uncurl, allowing the baby to roll onto the floor.

Throughout motherhood, sleep is continuously interrupted, through no fault of our own.

Then various relationships took place where sleeping was disrupted by other factors. There were times when they served a purpose, a great purpose, but afterward there is no need to draw out the agony of trying to achieve a restful slumber. What is the point? Sure, a cuddle and loving embrace is sweet, but it wakes me up again. Once that happens, forget falling asleep, I'm back to listening to the snoring. To avoid the turn and spoon action, I would lie on the far edge of the mattress, holding on for dear life, and pray the sun would come up earlier than expected. To complement the restful night, I now had to contend with rat maze hair and puffy eyes. Honestly, I wonder why they still kept wanting to stay over. I eventually became selfish and came up with reasons not to have sleep-overs. An early morning appointment, a sore stomach or medication I needed to take, were my prime excuses.

I'd go home, embrace my bed, and drift off for as long as my circadian rhythm allowed. Bliss!

Today, the pattern revolves around two to three-hour stints, awake for a couple of hours and return to sleep for around four hours. I suppose I have my six to seven hours sleep, but they are interrupted. At least there is silence and I'm not having to contend with sleeping next to an East Link boring machine.

THE GROUP CHAT

The idea of staying in contact with others is lovely, however it can become a nightmare. I was inadvertently included in a group chat with several school friends from my graduating year. The reunions are bearable and at least there is an option to join the event if you'd like. This group chat came about as my dear friend (also a school friend) had an encounter with one of the old girls. They reminisced and asked after everyone's health and circumstances. At the conclusion, the old friend vowed to put together a group chat so we could all remain in touch. My details were handed over and hence I was alerted that I had been added to the chat.

The first DING began,

Hi everyone. Great to be in contact with you all. Wishing Sarah a happy birthday on Friday. 🎂 🎂

I had a gut instinct this would not end well.

Have a wonderful special day 🩶 Laura dinged her best wishes.

Enjoy your special day Michelle joined the mounting dingers.

Buzz. *Hip hip hooray Sarah. Best wishes* Clare added.

By this stage I had clicked the phone to silent but as I own an Apple Watch, every notification vibrates on my wrist to alert me of the incoming message.

By the evening, there were twenty birthday wishes for Sarah. As yet I hadn't contributed as I thought I didn't want to get involved with all this back and forth. It was already irritating. The thought of twenty other birthdays that would be acknowledged, plus all other irrelevant messages that would emerge sent a tremor of horror through me. I wanted out.

By the end of the evening, Sarah forwarded her message.

Thanks for all your birthday wishes. I've had a great day. John took me and the kids to Noosa for a staycation. Just beautiful with gorgeous weather. Couldn't have asked for a better birthday .

After about ten minutes, the birthday wishes had evolved into Noosa notices.

Looovvve Noosa .

I was in Noosa for Christmas.

Gorgeous, where are you staying?

Brian and I are heading there next month ✈.

I couldn't stand it. I was edging closer to throwing my watch against the wall.

I didn't know what to do. I didn't ask to be in the group and I was in the middle of it. In the end I sent a birthday wish to Sarah as I saw that on WhatsApp everyone can see who is on the chat. I felt rude if I didn't at least acknowledge her "special" day. I felt like saying, "Before you know it, the next birthday will be coming around." I refused to be part of the Noosa commentary team. One more emoji and I'd scream.

I looked up how to step away from a chat without being noticed and you can't. If you choose to leave the chat, the person who set it up will be notified. How would that look? I persevered with the dings for as long as I could. I vowed I would not access each notification, not open the app. That way, the girls may think, I wasn't seeing the messages and not be expecting a response.

I sat back and wondered why I was wasting so much energy and time trying to figure this out.

By the next week, another birthday down, a child's wedding congratulations, a perfect brownie recipe shared, I was at my wits end. The incessant dinging was mind numbing. If you enjoy the constant frivolous banter, then good for you. Two weeks was my limit. I tried, I really did. This old girl is out! Silence.

GYM OR GIN?

This can be a dilemma for many women. Can you have both gym and gin in your life?

We know that fitness is vital as we age, but so is reward.

"We deserve a good cheese platter," was my dear friend Cathy's response when I asked why she didn't attend her Pilates class that week.

"I couldn't say no to Ellie. It was her sixtieth," she reported.

"And the week before you didn't go either," I continued.

"I know. A big G n T night the night before. If I had lain down on one of their Pilate beds, I promise you, you wouldn't have been able to pry me off."

"Perhaps a Zumba class would have worked instead," I offered as a tongue in cheek alternative.

We work hard at justifying the reasons why we enjoy the simple pleasures in life. Can't I balance the gym and gin? The perfect gym membership should include an optional gin and tonic upon arrival. They would have lots of early arrivals, I assure you. Having gin running through your veins would incentivise and energise any class you attended. I would be bending and stretching without grunting or pleading for help. The spring in the step it would provide would loosen not only the joints but also the tongue. I'm sure I'd be much more friendly and fun loving in class. At the conclusion of each session, another G n T would be offered for those of us who wished to remain limber and laughing. At this rate, I would have made a few more friends, and vowed to meet the following week and continue the fun and frivolity.

With the prices these gyms charge, I'm certain they won't go into liquidation over a couple of drinkies. My inhibitions would dissipate and I would even bring out the leotards that would end up looking like Pamela Anderson's, because they, like hers, would be way too small for me now. With extra rolls and fadoobadaas, I'd be laughing all the way back to the gym bar for another G n T.

Watch the memberships go through the roof. Add a selection of wines and mini charcuterie boards for post "workout" and you have achieved the perfect balance. Gym and gin. Everyone goes home and pours themselves a glass of wine, anyway.

Texting and the elderly citizen is another story. The other day my mother replied to my text after an hour, which is unusual, as her replies are normally swift. There were a series of irrelevant and disjointed letters that had no semblance to any words. As a response, my immediate thought was, she has had an episode, an embolism, or perhaps a minor stroke. But she was trying to contact me. This is where my mind goes with a frail, ninety-year-old mother who lives alone. Not even a minute later she texts me again, "Not sure what my last message said, I can't even recall writing or sending it. A mystery." *There is no mystery Mum, you wrote it and you sent it,* I wanted to say. *It happens, but kudos to you for being able to text.*

Texting is the perfect communication avenue for an introverted person like myself. A drawn-out phone conversation is more trouble than it's worth; I'll just text. You get in and get out. No need to linger, explain the background story, the outcome, the complex reasoning behind the message, just use the least number of words needed and so be it. I have friends who like to write an essay or a short story when they text, a puff piece full of extra information and opinion I couldn't care less about. They occasionally end with a, "so how are you?" By that stage, I'm so exhausted, having read the article, my vision has blurred and I need a rest.

I reply with a few words which I'm sure would be questioned, "Are these all the words you can spare?"

That's one group of friends. Then there are friends who, for coolness or lack of time, can't or won't write my full Christian name. Instead, the writing resembles that of a foreign language student, with a series of unconnected letters. Over time my name, Patrizia, had been whittled down to one letter. In these texts I'm referred to as "P". Is it too much to ask you to write my name in full please? Can you spare the one to two seconds it might take? Then there is the TY, K, IDK, OMG, LMK, BC, LOL. To get to where an OK is halved to just K, says it all. I have to put up with TK instead of thank you, IDK instead of I don't know, OMG instead of oh my god, LMK instead of let me know, BC instead of because and LOL instead of just saying, "that was funny" rather than laugh out loud. When I see my abbreviated name, I can't help but think of going to the toilet, it conjures that image for me. I'm a visual person, so please stop calling me "P".

Dame Edna's impressive words of wisdom: "I must admit, like most women approaching middle age, unfortunately, I'm approaching it from the wrong direction."

Everything is just fine like this, thank-you.

I'm fascinated by people's lives especially those who are involved in the mafia or recently, the *Real Housewives* franchise, mind you, not all the housewives. Beverley Hills, New York, Salt Lake, New Jersey and Atlanta are entertaining. I like to imagine myself slotting into the lives of either of these rich and vacuous women, or the wives of the dangerous mafia bosses. Being raised in an honest, law-abiding, conservative household, contemplating the complete antithesis of my life is intriguing. Being a mob wife, I could focus on insignificant routines, such as, girls' lunches and trips, hair appointments, facials, spas and shopping. Who could complain? To be consumed with these obligations rather than the cooking, ironing, washing, vacuuming, and grocery shopping would be a delight. I would much rather only be concerned about my husband returning home with all ten fingers and no bullet holes. I think I've watched too many mob movies.

Being a housewife would entail

having a glamour squad follow me everywhere. How would that be? Getting up in the morning looking like I've just been dragged along a dirt road and pronounced road kill, then being transformed into a fully coiffed, made-up glamour puss dressed in high fashion top to toe. I know the shows are scripted, however, yelling and having hissy fits all the while talking behind each other's back, seems like a fun way of making millions of dollars. I realise that you will all be aghast at these comments, but I am sixty-six and allowed to give my opinion. Many women would never contemplate the invasive nature of the cameras in their lives for a period of time each year, but if I'm looking good and being invited to beautiful locations to film, I'd make an effort. Remember the other option? Road-kill.

Joy

My dearest friend and I came up with our mantra for 2024. It was JOY. We were determined to find joy in our lives. Do things which brought us joy. We planned to be surrounded by people emanating joy and take part in joyful activities.

As the fireworks filled our skies at the stroke of midnight, we were filled with hope and enthusiasm for the coming twelve months. What exciting and joyous times would be ahead? Did anyone predict that this tiny word, joy, would be filled with too much expectation?

The new year resolution theory is a farce. In my younger years, I made a few. The typical resolutions of losing weight, drinking less, all fell on deaf expectations. I failed miserably on all counts and made a new year resolution to not make new year resolutions. Just let things flow. The joy was squeezed out of me when I tumbled onto that foyer floor in Amsterdam, looking like a drunken fool. Joy was missing when I, along with my family, waved goodbye to the family home after its sale. Along with complete obliteration of any sign of joy coming from my mother, I felt that this newly formed tradition was about to see its last day. Goodbye joy and hello reality.

Having now entered 2025, my search for joy will come from within. I will find joy in the small things. The joy of having moments to myself, of sharing a coffee with friends, having a wine with my daughter at our favourite local wine bar, talking about travel (just talking about it brings joy) and appreciating each day that does not bring a health concern. I will concede to a mixture of joy and reality.

THE NEW YORK PAD

My New York pad is no more. I'm not speaking of an actual apartment in New York, (if only) rather my apartment where I live in Melbourne. I had taken much joy in furnishing my top-floor apartment and decided a black, white and gold accessory palette would lend itself to an elegant and sophisticated environment. I loved it. When my daughter saw the photos of the newly decorated space, she exclaimed, "Mum, it looks like a New York apartment." That was the best compliment I could have received and, as a huge admirer of New York and an avid interior stylist, I was thrilled to have been able to create a space that resembled my idol, NYC.

Fast forward to today, add one daughter and one cat as occupiers since the redecoration and the once pristine cream boucle couch now looks like a hairy, unkempt, second-hand piece of furniture you'd find dumped on the curb. Strings, lumps, and protrusions all need a serious haircut. Please don't think that the cat has been denied any scratching areas. He's had upright posts, lay flat scratchers, inclined scratchers, a three-storey cat house encircled with scratching fabrics. Alas no, it's the couch that gets priority beating plus my grey fabric bed frame. The cat lies on his side on the floor and with his paws does a scratch and glide at the same time as he circumnavigates the perimeter of the couch as if he were Spider-Cat. All my daughter can say is, "Isn't he cute?"

Granted, he is cute, but the cuteness is going to be to the detriment of one good looking apartment. I now have a three-storey tower in the corner of the open lounge for His Cuteness to make use of. He has a box of toys which you will find scattered around the floor. My beautiful black velvet studded armchair has a huge fluffy throw to protect it from the cute destructive claws. This is one piece he will not ruin. Then there are eating vessels for different purposes, slow eating, medium eating and normal eating, for goodness' sake. Blankets folded in different corners to allow for sleeping choice. This cat has taken over the space, slowly but surely. I adore him, and that makes it difficult to feel resentment for losing my pristine area.

As my daughter says, "He's my son." How can this grandmother deny her grand-cat the luxuries of life?

My transparency and clarity of thought regarding needing a male partner, or significant other or mere friend, whatever label you wish to attach to it, is consistent. There is no need to feel the pressure of having one. However, IF I were to come across a man who piqued my interest, he would have to fit into certain categories. He would need to be independently wealthy. I'm not putting up with funding anyone else's lifestyle – once bitten, twice shy. He would need to be taller than me and with my height of five foot eight inches, that is not too much to ask. He would need a great sense of humour. This would be the biggest draw card as I intend on spending a great deal of time laughing and joking together. Next are arms and legs. Now these are a feature I am attracted to in a man. Strong arms and muscular legs, a symbol of strength and protection. Preferably, no tattoos. In my age bracket, I haven't found men to be as tattooed as their younger counterparts. I would grow tired of looking at the same picture show.

I know myself. A good head of hair is preferable, but not essential.

Manners are a must. There is no allowance for disrespect of any kind. A tight bum would be nice, but given mine isn't up to scratch anymore, I can't be too picky. To top off my list, my requests are for either childless and amicably divorced, or never married. The latter may be a cause for concern, however, seeing I was only married for nine years, I can't be too critical there either. A man who likes to travel is necessary as I intend to spend more time doing this.

Last but not least, a sexually active yet not maniacal man is the icing on the cake. He needs to be prepared for sleeping separately most nights, as he will have his own home to reside in, and I will keep mine. In conclusion, a funny, wealthy, tall, polite, handsome, traveller, who has great arms and strong legs, never married and childless with a tightish arse, happy to have the occasional romp in the hay but then retreat to his own home should be a breeze to find. Not too much to ask, seeing that I'm so perfect. It would help if I were actually looking.

DRAWING TO A CLOSE

As I draw to a close, I conclude that life is a wonderful thing at any age. But we still need to laugh. I think about my future. What about my seventies and eighties and nineties, if I get there? Will I finally give in to Botox? The high heels, will they make a reappearance? The bright red lips: will they return? Could I start dating a younger man? Even one month younger? Whatever happens, I will approach it with a sense of humour and a smile. My experience with my mother has taught me that focusing on the negative aspects of life is unproductive, both for yourself and those around you. I will do my utmost not to burden anyone else with my issues and hold on dearly to my BFFs. That is all that I need. As long as I have my Prosecco and Twisties, life is good!

I enjoy being sixty-six... I find it relaxing. I can say no to many things. I don't want to change or grow, what for? What you should do compared to what you would or could do is very different. I'm crossing my fingers that I will be able to do things I want to do more often and not just those I should.

How many times have I heard advice that goes like this? *You shouldn't listen to the negativity, shouldn't watch the news, shouldn't let it affect you.* Aren't you tired of being told what you shouldn't do? I've lived sixty-six years and of course I could have done some things differently... I would have made other decisions if I knew what lay ahead. The benefit of hindsight. In retrospect, what I should or shouldn't have done is irrelevant. The aim now is living my best life, the way I want to and loving doing so.

It has taken some time, considerable patience and positive self-talk to conclude that the aging process affects every single woman in different ways. *Vive la différence.* However, we arrive at the same endpoint. Throughout my life I focused on being on trend, fashion forward perhaps, but definitely fashion conscious. Coming from a heritage of well put together women in my family, it was innate to follow suit. Today my focus is on family and the fashion trends are coming and going without my even taking note. It is an enlightening feeling. I feel confident within myself, and I'm at peace with how I've aged, accepting both the good and the not-so-good. I continue to believe every decade in a woman's life is unique. We evolve and change over time, thank goodness. With this upcoming decade, I will focus on health and happiness. I will remain fashionable but not fixated. It's a wonderful age, sixty-six, an age of consent.

I consent to speaking up, not putting up with people or situations that will not drive me forward and I absolutely consent to saying “NO” more often. This will be for self-preservation and self-respect and to those who don’t understand that reasoning, I say, move along.

My dear readers, we are in it together. Women supporting each other, women aging and seeing the funny side as we hold hands and slide down this aging hill together.

Hugs and kisses

Xoxo

www.ingramcontent.com/pod-product-compliance
Lightning Source LLC
Chambersburg PA
CBHW021825090726
47818CB00077BA/48

* 9 7 8 1 7 6 4 6 5 1 4 2 4 *